Tartan Turmoil
fall&rise
of SCOTTISH FOOTBALL

by

Kevin Gallacher

To John
Best Wishes

Tartan Turmoil
fall&rise
of SCOTTISH FOOTBALL

Published in 2006 by 90 Minutes Publications
Eanam Wharf, Blackburn, Lancs BB1 5BL
www.90minutesltd.co.uk

ISBN 0-9546251-5-3

Designed and Printed by Mercer Print
Star Works, Newark St. Accrington, Lancs BB5 0BP

Introduction

Like many players in my time as Scotland Manager, Kevin Gallacher wore the Scottish jersey with pride. Like me, he was involved with the Scotland set-up at a time, especially with hindsight, that is seen by many as one of the best. I was lucky enough, and privileged enough, to have players like Kevin at my disposal. And rest assured, he and others from that era never gave less than 110% to the Scottish cause. Also the likes of Colin Hendry, Ally McCoist, David Weir, Gary McAllister, Paul McStay, Tommy Boyd, Jim Leighton, Andy Goram, Colin Calderwood, Stuart McCall, Craig Burley, John Collins and Christian Dailly.

It is no different with this, Kevin's autobiographical look at Scottish Football over the last 30 years. He pulls no punches and says it as he sees it. Everyone would agree that, my old friend Walter Smith has a big task on his hands to get Scottish Football back up the world rankings. The fact that we are at our lowest level ever since the rankings came into effect, speaks for itself. How we arrived in this position has been well covered in this book and Kevin has been able to call on anyone who has been anyone in Scottish football for his views.

This is a forthright and honest endeavour to look at why the late 80s and early 90s were so successful and why the last five years or so have seen a steady decline in our fortunes. Some of the answers are surprising, but looking on the bright side - things can only get better!

Kevin Gallacher was an extremely talented footballer but, more importantly, he was, and is, a man of integrity and substance. His book reflects, in candid manner, the strength of feeling he has for Scottish football.

Craig Brown CBE

Contents

chapter one

THE WORLD CUP
FINALS 1998

Imagine the scene. It was a red hot summer's day in Paris, the sweat was running down my forehead, the adrenalin was flowing, and I was running and chasing every ball. All of a sudden, the ball was knocked down in the box. I was sharp and alert and ready to sprint for the ball. I had just pushed off, when suddenly I felt a hand on my back. There was enough contact for me to fall over and as I hit the ground, I looked around to see what the outcome had been. What was the referee going to give? I heard the whistle blow, the referee ran towards the penalty spot, the players congregating beside him, and it was at that moment I knew that I had won Scotland a penalty kick that could get us back into the match with the world champions Brazil.

At that point in the game, we were behind to a goal from Sampaio who had opened the scoring early from a headed corner. Here we were, on the brink of getting an equaliser. It was a nerve-racking moment, with everyone looking at each other thinking and wondering who was going to take the penalty kick! Gary MacAllister

was the usual penalty taker and, although he did travel with the squad for the tournament, he was not fit. It's pure speculation now, but after his miss-fortune of that penalty against England at Wembley in euro '96, would he have got up to take this one? Would he have been the right person?

It seemed like a life time, but was probably only about thirty seconds, before the lonely figure of John Collins calmly stepped out from the crowd of players and walked up towards the penalty spot with the ball under his arm. He looked very cool and confident, and he placed the ball on the spot, stood back, his chest sticking out like a proud peacock and he stared at the Brazilian goalkeeper, Taffarel. The players from both sides were now at the edge of the box, jostling for the best positions, ready to follow in the Collins shot, in case Taffarrel got a hand to it and there was a rebound. I was standing as if ready for a 100 metres sprint race, and took a quick glance around. I was looking at all the others and then I took one more look towards Collins. I could not believe how calm he looked but deep down, how nervous was he? I was a bag of nerves, and deep down so was he, I am positive about that. The referee blew his whistle, and Collins started his run up to the ball. Everyone by now was getting nervy and getting ready to follow the shot in. They needn't have bothered. In a flash, left footed, he placed the ball past Taffarrel. The goal got us back into the game. It was now 1-1 and with a lot of time left to play, this became our World Cup Final.

The opening game to the 1998 World Cup Finals, what an experience it was for me. It all started two years earlier in the qualifying rounds. Having qualified from the group stages we were now waiting to see who we would get in the draw.

Then amid all the excitement, there it was for everyone to see, we had been drawn in the same group as World Champions Brazil, alongside Norway and Morocco. The match against Brazil was to be the opening game of the 1998 World Cup; it would be played in the new stadium, The Stade de France on the 10th of June 1998. A newly built stadium for the competition and would have a maximum capacity and millions of TV viewers.

This was unbelievable. I was going to be playing against the World Champions in the opening game of a World Cup, my first World Cup match after missing out on the 1990 tournament. Brazil would have the likes of Ronaldo, Rivaldo, Cafu, Dunga, Aldair and Roberto Carlos - all household names in the world of football, and I was going to be playing a big part in trying to help Scotland beat them.

The Scotland squad had been announced and to everyone's amazement two hugely influential players were missing, Gary McAllister and Ally McCoist. Both were injured and unable to prove their fitness and neither was selected. With 'Coisty' not making the squad, Scott Booth was brought in to replace him and this opened the door for me to get the chance to start the first game. I had finished top scorer for Scotland in the qualifying rounds and this could mean a major role upfront for me to play. I was very, very excited.

Kevin Gallacher's World Cup jersey from the Brazil game in France 1998, signed by the Scotland Squad

We arrived in St Remi where we were based for the majority of our stay in France. The rain was falling and this was meant to be the start of summer. The funny thing was, John Collins having been living and playing in Monaco was telling me on the flight over to France that St Remi was one of the warmest and driest places in the south of France. Yet we arrived and not a ray of sunshine to be seen it was like Scotland really, I felt at home! As the big day got closer, the sun started to get warmer and the humidity was increasing. I desperately wanted to get out in the sun, but my pale complexion made this impossible, I couldn't risk sunburn so close to the big game.

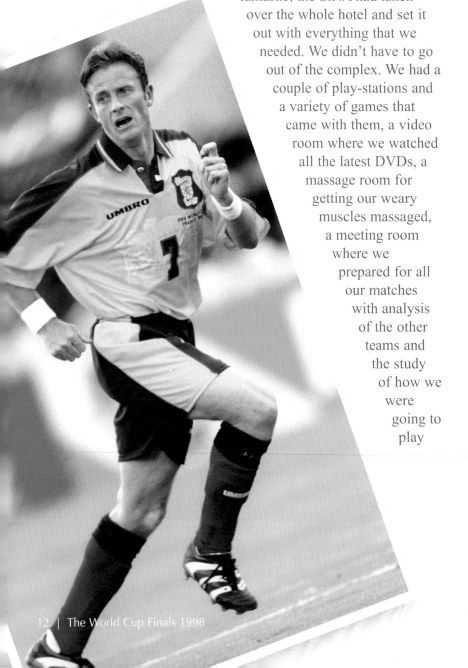

The hotel was absolutely fantastic; the S.F.A had taken over the whole hotel and set it out with everything that we needed. We didn't have to go out of the complex. We had a couple of play-stations and a variety of games that came with them, a video room where we watched all the latest DVDs, a massage room for getting our weary muscles massaged, a meeting room where we prepared for all our matches with analysis of the other teams and the study of how we were going to play

before and after the team had been announced. On top of that, we had an indoor and an outdoor pool for relaxing in and a room that was made into a very small gym containing barbells and dumbbells.

Having prepared all week to adjust to the heat, it was now time for us to head off to Paris and get the last day's preparation done before the big match. Arriving at The Stade de France on the Friday night, we had a look at this magnificent arena and had our last training session before the big day. As you can imagine, a good night's sleep was on the cards, but unfortunately the butterflies were too much and Colin Hendry and I spent a fortune on phone calls making sure all our families and friends had arrived safely and settled into the villas that they were all staying in. Most importantly, we were checking that they had their tickets for the match. After a couple of visits to the loo, a late night movie and a chat about the game, we both eventually managed to go to sleep.

Waking up for breakfast, after what seemed like a ten minute nap, I was feeling completely knackered, as though I just wanted to go back to sleep. Then reality dawned, one of the biggest moments of my life was only a few hours away. I took a cool shower and after having my breakfast it was time for our final team meeting. With everyone congregating in the meeting room, we sat down and had a chat. The nerves were already starting to show, when manager Craig Brown ran through all the tactics for the game, so that everyone knew what he had to do. We then went back to our rooms, to get ready for the journey to the stadium. We had a sponsorship from a kilt maker from Inverness and our big surprise for the Tartan Army was that we intended to wear them on our arrival at the stadium (as no other national side had ever worn the kilt before) and once inside have a walk around the pitch showing them off to all the supporters. When we were approaching the stadium the crowd

COUPE DU MONDE

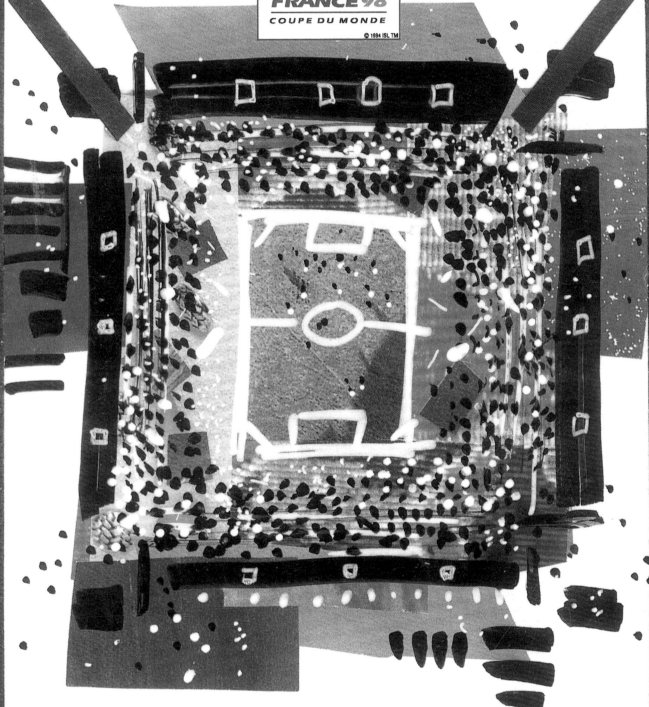

FRANCE 98

Tartan Turmoil
the fall and rise of Scottish Football

© 1997 ISL

reaction was unbelievable. Outside, the majority of the Tartan Army that had arrived early, were singing and dancing and with their faces painted with the Scottish Saltier it looked like something out of the film Braveheart.

Once we were inside the stadium, we walked out on to the pitch showing off our Kilts to the sponsors and to the supporters who had gone into the stadium early. After what seemed like fifteen minutes, and after some of the lads had a brief word with their families, the promotion work was done and because it was so hot, it was back to the dressing room and into the air-conditioned atmosphere to prepare for the serious business ahead.

As you entered the dressing room, the numbered jerseys were all hanging up on specific lockers, the kit bags in a neat pile in the corner of the room. The tactics board was up for you to look at and lots of people seemed to be walking all over the place. The kilts were very heavy and the weather was boiling hot, and most of the guys wanted to get them off as soon as they could, just to cool down. I sat down at my allocated spot, underneath the number 7 jersey and slowly started to take it all in. All the lads had different routines and I was no different! I would start by taping my feet up, to prevent my feet getting blisters, John Collins would start with a muscle massage, and Jim Leighton would put his contact lenses in. There were so many different things to do, so many different superstitions.

Then, there was a knock on the dressing room door. It was the chairman of the SFA, Bill Dickie, arriving to wish us well. He told Craig Brown that there were a couple of gentlemen outside and they

Tartan Turmoil
the fall and rise of Scottish Football

would like to come into the dressing room to see the players. Craig Brown then asked the boys if it was allright if Sean Connery and Billy Connolly could come in and wish us well for the match. Not surprisingly, the lads agreed to this, as it is not that often that you get to meet these guys. Just when it all seem sorted, they were not allowed in as they did not have any security passes, so the stewards would not let them through. Many top celebrities ranging from pop stars to film stars had come to the match to give us some moral support.

The opening ceremony was taking place out on the playing surface, so we had to do a warm up indoors in a room that measured about 20 feet wide by 20 feet wide with pillars down the middle. A little bit of jogging and a stretch was all you were capable of, then out to a corridor 30 feet long by 4 feet wide to do all the sprinting work. Well you can imagine 22 Scots lads running around trying to avoid each other while across in the other corridor were the samba dancing Brazilians.

The referee's whistle blew and his assistant entered the dressing room to check our studs and see if we were wearing any jewellery. It was then time to line up in the tunnel. As the lads made their way, one by one, to the tunnel area, Colin Calderwood was doing his final preparations like slapping his face and shouting "come on Scotland". Lunatic that he was, he then raced out of the dressing room turning the wrong way down the corridor before realising and turning back to go towards the tunnel. All of this was caught on the video technician, Brian Hendry's, video camera and shown to all the players at the next team meeting with a few other funnies to keep our moral going.

We lined up side by side with the Brazilians. They were being led out by their captain, Dunga, and we were led out by my big room partner Colin Hendry. Standing across from me was Roberto

Carlos, and I remember thinking I couldn't believe how small he was. By now though, everything was starting to get hazy, and I was concentrating hard on what I had to do in the game. You could hear the crowd roaring and that in itself told me that the atmosphere outside was going to be absolutely electrifying. Walking out of the tunnel and looking around such a magnificent arena, was an experience of a lifetime. What with the red, the blues and tartan colours around one half of the ground and the gold colours of the Brazilian supporters at the other, added to by the ticker tape and the fire works going off it was a magnificent spectacle and the most nerve wracking experience ever. We made our way onto the pitch and lined up for the National anthems, the hairs on the back of my neck standing up as I gave it my best vocals. I was trying to take all of this in so I would remember such an unbelievable occasion. The match kicked off and as we all know, we eventually lost the game 2-1, but I think we did ourselves proud!

I think for the record a resume of that game is well worth while – it was after all one of Scotland's best ever performances, even in defeat, and was possibly the pinnacle of an era which as a nation we will do well to achieve again in the near future.

Report courtesy of the Scottish Daily Herald
Brazil 2, Scotland 1

The World Cup fates, it seems, must always conspire against Scotland just as they did yesterday when the national side were defeated by the cruellest of own goals by Celtic captain Tom Boyd.

There were only 18 minutes remaining of the opening game when the Scots suffered that bitter blow which now makes qualification to the second stage of these finals very difficult.

Before that, Craig Brown's team had fought back after losing a goal to the

world champions with only four minutes of the game played. They had refused to crumble when that happened, and eight minutes before half time, John Collins had equalised from the penalty spot and for long spells the Scottish team played with the confidence they had demonstrated in the two friendly games in the United States.

They refused to be overawed, refused to accept the role the team had been given as mere cannon fodder for the South Americans.

This was a team which performed with some style and one which contributed to making the first match of these finals the kind of spectacle the organisers had wanted.

And, yet, once more, when glory was within their grasp it was snatched away, and Tom Boyd, blameless for the goal, will be distraught that he was the man whose last touch sent the ball over the line to send his nation to defeat.

It was not Boyd's fault. It was not anyone's fault. It was that twist of fate which has dogged Scotland international teams in all the World Cups I have watched over the last 24 years.

The killer goal came at a period of the match when the Scots had settled into the passing game which they have developed over the years that Craig Brown has been in charge.

Brazil had made changes in that second half as they had failed to penetrate the Scotland defence, and as a draw began to look the most likely result of all.

If the coach, Mario Zagallo, had lost out to Zico in the pre-game team selection, he won the war on the bench when he restored the two players he had wanted in from the beginning. Leonardo replaced one of Zico's men, Giovanni, at the beginning of the second period and then Denilson took over from the other, Bebeto, with 20 minutes remaining.

The appearance of Denilson lifted the champions for a vital few minutes and it was then the goal came. Cafu burst forward from the right wing back position into the penalty box, evading a challenge from Gordon Durie as he did so. He struck a shot for goal, Jim Leighton made a superb stop, but the ball then struck Boyd as he raced in to help the keeper and bounced from him over the line where Colin Hendry stood helpless.

The Scottish captain crawled into the back of the net to retrieve the ball and the expression on his face told the whole sad old story.

John Collins scores against Brazil in France from the penalty spot

However, while they lost the game, the Scots left the Stade de France with an enhanced reputation.

The Tartan Army who acclaimed them afterwards knew that too. They knew in their hearts that their team had been desperately close to achieving one of the finest results in their country's history and they recognised that the players, all 13 of them who were used, had not let them down.

Lesser men would have given up after the fourth minute goal. A team with less confidence in their system would have panicked and changed. Scotland's players did neither.

Instead they re-grouped and within 10 minutes of the opener they were pushing the ball about patiently.

The goal had been a disaster, coming as it did, before the Scots had settled properly. Rivaldo swung in a corner from the left and Craig Burley failed to pick up Cesar Sampaio who reached the ball at the near post and guided his header into the net.

Soon, though, the Scots were going forward defiantly, sweeping the ball across the field, refusing to allow the Brazilians possession. When Brazil burst into attack Jim Leighton was there, making saves from Rivaldo and from Roberto Carlos and from Ronaldo.

But at the other end of the field Gordon Durie's ability in the air, Kevin Gallacher's pace and Darren Jackson's persistence were forcing the Brazilians into mistakes. One of these came after 36 minutes when Sampaio barged down Gallacher in the penalty box when it looked as if the ball

was going to run through to Taffarel at the end of a Scottish attack.

The Spanish referee gave the penalty, waved away Brazilian protests, and a minute later John Collins stepped up to strike the ball low past the veteran Brazilian keeper.

How the Tartan Army celebrated - and how the Brazilian supporters were suddenly muted. Then Aldair was cautioned for a tackle from behind on Gallacher. That meant Brazil had had two men yellow carded while Scotland had just one, Darren Jackson, who was cautioned for touchline challenge on Dunga after 24 minutes.

There were anxious moments for Scotland at the start of the second half when they conceded two corners in the opening few minutes but they survived and soon Taffarel stopped a Dailly shot as the Scots attempted to step up the tempo.

A flowing move which began with Durie and involved Gallacher, Lambert and then

Gallacher again ended with a low ball whipping dangerously across the face of the Brazilian goal and Cafu widly cleared for a corner at the far post.

Taffarel stopped a Burley drive, was put under pressure from Durie and then just as the Scottish players looked comfortable again the roof fell in when Brazil scored their second.

Following that Billy McKinlay replaced Jackson and towards the end Tosh McKinlay took over from Christian Dailly.

The changes brought a late flurry and Gallacher and Durie shot over and Taffarel stopped another Burley try but, sadly, the damage had been done and could not be repaired.

Manager Craig Brown had taken a brave gamble by trying to attack the world champions and it almost paid off for him.

But no amount of pre-match planning can legislate for the misfortunes which lie in wait to ambush Scotland's World Cup dreams.

Next it's Norway in Bordeaux and what the Scots need is a result similar to the one they had against Sweden in Italy in the l994 finals. They do deserve to get that.

Brazil - Taffarel, Cafu, Aldair, Roberto Carlos, Junior Baiano, Dunga, Cesar Sampaio, Rivaldo, Giovanni, Ronaldo, Bebeto. Substitutes - Germano, Ze Roberto, Andre Cruz, Goncalves, Ze Carlos, Doriva, Leonardo, Denilson, Emerson, Edmundo, Dida.

Scotland - Leighton, Burley, Calderwood, Hendry, Boyd, Lambert, Collins, Dailly, Jackson, Gallacher, Durie. Substitutes - Sullivan, Gould, B McKinlay, Weir, Elliott, T McKinlay, Whyte, McNamara, Gemmill, Booth, Donnelly.

Referee - J M Garcia Aranda (Spain).

Beaten - but every player was a winner
by Jim Reynolds

Jim Leighton: No chance with the goal after just five minutes, and he kept Scotland in the game in the first half with magnificent saves from Roberto Carlos and Ronaldo. I doubt if any keeper will be more unlucky than Leighton was 18 minutes from time. He did all he could, yet watched in horror as the ball bounced back off Tom Boyd.

Colin Calderwood: A solid performance and calm when Scotland came under pressure. When the Brazilians were at their most dangerous, he made some excellent and vital tackles.

Colin Hendry: Played a captain's part and looked fully in command. He was solid on the ground and magnificent in the air, winning almost everything.

Tom Boyd: He had a difficult job to do, but, like Hendry and Calderwood, coped well with the threat of Ronaldo. He had no chance when the ball cannoned off him to give Brazil their winning goal. He has the character to put that behind him.

Craig Burley: Has been telling us that he is not a wing back or a right back, and was proved right, especially when poor marking by him and Collins at the near post caused the first goal. However, he settled well after that and looked good going forward.

Paul Lambert: Always in space to help his mates. His experience at the top level in Europe showed here. He seldom wasted a ball and brought the calming influence needed in front of the back three. Probably Scotland's most accomplished player.

John Collins: A typical professional performance and he showed tremendous composure, under great pressure, when firing in the penalty. Collins was on a par with anyone in the midfield area last night.

Christian Dailly: The occasion looked a bit much for the youngster. A couple of poor touches early on did nothing for his confidence. He

Scotland's Kevin Gallacher holds off Morocco's Noureddine Naybet

Brazil's Denilson celebrates their 2nd goal

Tartan Turmoil
the fall and rise of Scottish Football

played better in the second half although he could not keep Cafu busy enough. Was replaced by Tosh McKinlay.

Darren Jackson: Had the doubtful distinction of being given the first yellow card of the tournament. Generally did the job he was asked to do which was chase and harry, but posed no threat inside the box. Was replaced by Billy McKinlay.

Kevin Gallacher: Had an excellent match, especially in the first half when his pace caused problems. It was one of those runs inside the box which forced Cesar Sampaio to panic and concede the penalty. Gallacher could have a good tournament.

Gordon Durie: As usual, worked and ran his heart out. His strength and running power caused the Brazilians several anxious moments, and this despite the fact that he did not get the best of service.

After the match, the Scottish security man Big Willie, as we knew him, rounded up our families at the rendezvous point and brought them to a room. It was the first time we had seen them in several weeks. Gary Mac went round and shook all the players' hands trying to lift our spirits. As we were all standing around talking to our families, 'Coisty' came up to me, shook my hand and asked me did I have his video on 'diving in the box'? I didn't know what he meant !!!!!!!

Scotland's Kevin Gallacher in battle with Norway's Vidar Riseth

As for Jim Reynold's comments that 'Gallacher could have a good tournament', I like to think in that game alone I did myself justice, even if future events with the draw against Norway and desperately disappointing defeat to Morroco, would see us fail again to get beyond the group stages. No one at that time would have thought it would be at least 2010 before a Scottish team would appear in the Finals again.

FRANCE 98

*Kevin Gallacher Player of the
Year 1979 Duntocher Boys Club*

chapter two

IN THE
BEGINNING

Kevin aged 11, Duntocher Boys Club

Looking back, it is easy to see now, why I went into football, and probably why I made a success of it. I have spoken to players and managers, proud to be Scottish, and with years of experience behind them. Their comments make interesting reading alongside my own experiences from a small lad until the present day.

I met with Walter Smith, the current Scotland Manager, up at the Scottish FA and asked him if changes in school football and higher standards of living were affecting today's game?

"Yes it has...And I think there are a couple of things that have occurred which have seriously affected the game at schoolboy level.

"Firstly, from the schools point of view, there is the recreational side of the game. There are simply not enough boys interested in the sport to play a full-scale game and secondly, there are perhaps only one-tenth of those who enjoy playing football today on a regular basis to what there was 20 years ago."

"There's a distinct lack of interest, I feel.

The vast majority of the football I played as a youngster was unstructured. We played anywhere - on the street, in the park, on wasteland, anywhere that was reasonably flat. I think the death of that type of 'get out and play' football has been the biggest influence in the non-production of footballers reaching a standard good enough to see them reach professional status."

Being brought up in a footballing family there was only one thing that I wanted to do, that of course was to play football.

Having a famous grandfather, Patsy Gallacher (ex Celtic, Falkirk and Ireland),

The modern game is based around a ball and four sets of coats.

David Moyes

Determination is what makes a kid succeed. Two kids of equal talent - one will fall by the wayside the other will go to a bigger club. You can manufacture a player and make them work hard for the team if they have the desire.

Graeme Souness

two uncles, Tommy and William Gallacher, and a cousin Stewart Gallacher, all having plied their trade as professional footballers, and my dad, Bernard, having participated at junior level, you could see in which direction I was destined to go.

For a young lad from a family of six, brought up in Clydebank, I knew this was going to be a hard but an enjoyable experience.

I had always wanted to go down the same route as my footballing idols, players like Kenny Dalglish, Joe Jordan, Jimmy 'Jinky' Johnston, Bobby Lennox and a whole lot more from that era. To go on and play alongside stars such as Paul Sturrock, Gordon Strachan, Ralph Milne, Charlie Nicholas, Ally McCoist and Mo Johnston but to name a few, was a dream come true. That was my boyhood dream and I was going to make it come true.

It all started at a very early age, as far back as I can remember. All I ever wanted to do was play with a ball. I would go out into the back garden and use the clothes poles as goalposts and would run around practising my twists and turns and shooting ability as well as my commentary skills, while being all of my idols in a one man football match.

I was the only youngster with a decent football, so I would always get asked around to the local green every evening after school, no matter what the weather was like for a kick-about. And my mum was often

swamped with loads of muddy clothes for washing, but as long as I enjoyed it, I don't think she really minded.

Then, one day at the age of ten, while I was in my dad's pub, The Clyde Vaults, situated on a corner of Main Street in Bridgeton, my friend Brian asked if I would accompany him while he went for a trial with an under 14s football team which was just starting up.

The trial was to take place just around the corner from the pub, on the Glasgow Green football pitches. Brian's team was a man short for the game, so they asked me to make up the numbers.

I wasn't kitted out for a game of football, so wearing ski pants and a pair of wellies, I asked some of the other boys if anyone had a spare pair of trainers in my size that I could borrow.

Thankfully, I managed to get hold of a pair, though not quite my size. I took part in the match and did well. I was selected for the team.

There were, however, a couple of problems. Firstly, the team was based in Glasgow which meant a lot of travelling from Clydebank and secondly, the boys were all older and bigger than me.

I played in a couple of games after which my Dad arranged, with an old friend of his, for me to have a trial with a local boy's club based in Clydebank. Annoyingly for me, I turned up with my mum, Annie, on the wrong training night!

Fortunately, my dad managed to get me another trial with another local side, Duntocher Boy's Club, and at last my football career got underway.

Two years later, I was playing regularly for my secondary school team, St.Andrew's High in Clydebank and also for the local boy's guild team, St.Margaret's. This meant that occasionally I played in three games over the weekend, but I enjoyed it.

I played for my school on a Saturday morning and after the game our teacher, Mr McCulloch, would drop me off wherever the guild match was being staged that afternoon. Then it was back home, to rest up for my Sunday morning match for Duntocher Boy's Club.

St. Andrews High School Clydebank winners of the League and Cup In 1980/81

On top of it all, I still managed to represent my county school's teams, Dunbartonshire Boys up to the age of fifteen, and then Glasgow Boys until I left school at sixteen. This meant lots of trials and if selected, I played in one or two extra games each month with them.

In the early 1960s Craig Brown worked as a P.E. teacher at various schools. He taught at Linlathen Secondary, Harris Academy, and the Grove in Broughty Ferry but mainly at McAlpine Primary in the afternoons, while in the mornings he trained with Dundee. He was assisted by two other Dundee players Doug Houston and Terry Christie.

Doug went on to play for Rangers while Terry became a headmaster at Musselburgh Grammar and managed several clubs including Alloa Athletic.

Craig, Terry and Doug coached about 30 boys each. Every boy played in matches and remember there weren't any substitutes - everyone got a game, yes, everyone.

When soccer sevens came out, they started to have groups gathering for Saturday morning sessions. And sometimes all 90 boys were ready to play. They all got a game, despite the pitches on the school playing field which they used, being rather on the small side.

At the time, most people agreed that small sided games were the answer. They might have been for some - but you tended to get all the good players arranging games between themselves, leaving the others, and there were quite a few, to muck in together.

Professional football clubs were allowed to sign young players on a 'Schoolboy Contract' from the age of thirteen, which meant you could be associated with that club until the age of sixteen, at which point you would either be

> *When I went to Dundee United they only had two boys on 'S' Forms, one was Graeme Payne the other was Stevie Mellon. I watched many Sunday morning boys games. I've always believed in a Youth policy to rear your own players. At the time the Lord Provos of Dundee, John Letford, was manager and had some of the best players in the league.*
>
> **Jim McLean**

Raymond Walsh, captain of Duntocher Boys Club

released or offered an apprenticeship.

Most clubs could only afford to take on about six or seven youngster as apprentices. Every Saturday and Sunday there would be several scouts watching our matches, looking out for young talent, seeing if they could get hold of the best young players in the area.

If the scout thought you were good enough, he would take you along to his club during the school holidays and show you the stadium and training facilities. And I was surprised to learn that not all clubs had these, some had to hire public pitches to train on.

Those selected would also get involved in coaching sessions with other invited players. A series of practice matches were arranged and

---

Telephone: 041-554 2710

Registered Office, Celtic Park, Glasgow, G40 3RE

Registered No. 3487 Scotland

The Celtic Football and Athletic Company Ltd.

VAT Reg. No. 260 2974 61

CELTIC PARK
GLASGOW, G40 3RE

Directors:
Desmond White, C.A., *Chairman*
Thomas L. Devlin
James M. Farrell, M.A., LL.B.
Kevin Kelly

Wm. McNeill, M.B.E., *Manager*

9th JUNE, 1980.

Dear Kevin,

Your footballing ability has been recommended to us and we would, therefore, like to invite you to join us for coaching sessions, starting Tuesday, 15th July, at 1.30 p.m. at our training ground, Barrowfield.

You should report to Barrowfield at the above time, bringing along your training gear and football boots. If you cannot join us on that date, perhaps you would be good enough to telephone the undersigned, advising him of same.

Looking forward to seeing you.

Yours sincerely,

John Kelman.
J. Kelman,
Chief Scout.

with the manager and his coaching staff looking closely at everyone taking part, to see if there were any promising footballers good enough to make it at a higher level, there was a great chance for someone to make the breakthrough.

If they thought you were good enough, someone from the club would then officially contact your parents and try convince them that the club was the right one for their son to join.

That's how I managed to get involved with Dundee United. I had gone along for trials with Clydebank and Celtic, had the customary stadium tours with a few other clubs too, but one day while I was sitting in an office at Tannadice Park, my life suddenly changed for the best!

Along with my dad Bernard, and my uncle Tommy, I sat on one side of a desk, opposite to manager

Jim McLean, the club's legendary disciplinarian. Out of all the previous meetings I had with other managers, he was the one who sold his football club to me.

Signing schoolboy forms at the age of 13, I had at last stepped on the first rung of the footballing ladder. It was the start of a terrific rollercoaster career that would take me all over the world with my country, Scotland, into the English Premiership with Coventry City, Blackburn Rovers and Newcastle United, see me play with and against some of the greatest footballers in the game and above all, thoroughly enjoy some 20 years as a professional.

Starting my apprenticeship with Dundee United at the beginning of July 1983 was a very daunting task, having only left school three months earlier. But all of a sudden I was rubbing shoulders with some of the star players from the 1970s and '80s.

I remember vividly walking into the changing room at Tannadice to be introduced to the rest of the players. I felt my jaw drop down, just like I had been dumped on the floor, at the sight of all these international footballers. It was breathtaking.

All newly-signed apprentices were given jobs to do after training, whether it was washing, drying or folding training kit to cleaning the pro's boots and keeping the dressing room tidy, as well as washing down the shower area and marking out a football pitch for training on.

It was tedious at times, but it had to be done. I enjoyed it really, although being assigned to washing kit and dressing room duty was

Kevin Gallacher St. Andrews High School 1980/81

There needs to be a balance between the old Apprenterships and Academies ……. boys made the tea, swept up and cleaned the boots…. they were treated quite harshly by the professionals but I never heard anyone complain… the danger now is at Academies they feel they have arrived long before they have done anything.

Graeme Souness

KEVIN
GALLACHER

not so much the hardest job of all, it was arguably the longest.

We had to wash and dry all the kit (and there was a lot of it at times), roll it up and put it into the correct places, so that the professionals would have the correct gear to wear for the next scheduled training session. Then, when training was finished, we had to do it all again – and whilst we were waiting for the kit to dry, we had to clean out the shower room and sweep and wash the dressing room floors. It was painstaking, hard work at times, yet it was my first regular 9 till 5 job! Who said football was an easy life? All this hard graft for just £45 per week!!!!

The Tannadice club was blessed with a friendly, family atmosphere, but step out of line and you were disciplined, whether that was from the manager himself or from one of the top players who had their own discipline committee. You were always under scrutiny…this was just the start for me learning the discipline side of the game.

FACTFILE

JIM MCLEAN
(born 1937, Larkhall, South Lanarkshire)

Kevin Gallacher and Jim McLean

PLAYING CAREER

Jim was born into a working class family in Larkhall, Lanarkshire in the west of Scotland in 1937. He served his time as an apprentice joiner, a career he pursued part time while playing league football, not unusual amongst footballers in the 1950s and 1960s.

In 1956 he started his football career with Hamilton Academical, as an inside forward. He would later go on to play with Clyde, Dundee and Kilmarnock. Although never achieving the same playing success as his brother Tommy he made a total of 474 appearances, scoring 170 times.

He retired from his playing career in 1970, returning to Dundee as a coach in July that year.

DUNDEE UNITED

After coaching at Dens Park for 18 months, Dundee's rivals Dundee United offered him the position of manager to replace the retiring Jerry Kerr in December, 1971.

Jim accepted the offer and made the trip over the road to start his managerial career at Tannadice Park at the age of 34.

McLean immediately started a co-ordinated youth policy which was to produce many fine young players over the two decades which followed. In the short term, he used his knowledge of the Scottish scene to buy experienced players who would allow him to re-shape both the squad and the style of play in line with his approach to coaching.

Initially the club's league form was average, remaining mostly mid-table for the next few years. McLean's first hint of the success, he would later achieve was leading the club to its first Scottish Cup final in 1974 and, despite defeat, it proved an important psychological step in McLean's and the club's development. The success of the Cup run was built upon the following season with a finish of fourth place, the club's best finish in the Scottish First Division before league restructuring.

As McLean's youth policy began to bear

fruit, the first of a number of talented young players began to emerge. McLean decided that his team could mount a challenge for the League championship in 1978/79, something of which the club, who had long lived in the shadow of McLean's former employers and rivals Dundee, had never previously proved capable of but after a disappointing finish in the first season of the new Premier Division, United started to prove that they were serious contenders for domestic honours.

In December 1979, McLean guided his team to triumph in the League Cup and retained it a year later. McLean was gradually building the club's reputation in Europe, with impressive wins over sides like AS Monaco, Borussia Moenchengladbach, PSV Eindhoven, Anderlecht and Werder Bremen. The counter-attacking style which he had developed proving ideally suited to that stage.

THE 80S, AND LEAGUE AND EUROPEAN SUCCESS

Despite the progress he had made few believed that McLean and United were potential Premier Division champions. Alex Ferguson's Aberdeen at that time were an emerging force in addition to the Old Firm. At this time he acted as No.2 to the late, great Jock Stein as Scotland Manager.

Rangers, who had seen a decline in their fortunes over the previous few years, offered McLean the job as manager at Ibrox. McLean did in fact engage in early negotiations with the Glasgow giants, one of his main problems with the job offer was Rangers' policy of not signing Roman Catholics, a policy McLean found a ridiculous restriction for any employer as well has having signed many talented Catholics with Dundee United. Many of whom he hoped that, if he ever did accept another managers job, he would be able to sign for his new club.

Despite the Rangers chairman assuring him that this policy would be scrapped if he were to accept the job, McLean decided that he was happy at Dundee United, as well as his family being happily settled in the Broughty Ferry area of Dundee. Perhaps a rare action in professional football, especially in recent times, of putting loyalty and family before money. McLean turned down another offer from Newcastle United in June, 1984.

Following his team's League success in 1983, Dundee United made their debut in the European Cup. McLean's counter-attacking tactics paired with a pressuring style brought some memorable results in that year's European campaign. McLean inspired United to the semi-finals of that years competition, a penalty-kick denying them a place in the Final.

Three years later McLean would finally take the team to a European final, this time in the UEFA Cup. For the rest of his managerial career McLean would continue to secure United's high standing in domestic football, finishing outside the top four clubs only once. And taking the team to a further five Scottish Cup finals, unfortunately he was unable to manage his team past the final hurdle of the competition.

THE BOARD

The Dundee United board marked their debt to McLean by making him a director in 1984; four years later he became Chairman and Managing Director. He retained those joint responsibilities until stepping down as manager in July 1993, after a marathon reign of 21 years and seven months. He remained as Chairman throughout the 1990s.

The next two years leading up to my senior debut for Dundee United, were spent learning and digesting the game of football from some of the games' top coaches. Men like Jim McLean, Walter Smith, Gordon Wallace and Jimmy Bone were all trying to improve my ability, help increase my knowledge of the game, as well as trying to build up my scrawny frame, weighing in at just under 9 stone.

FACTFILE
WALTER SMITH
(born February 24, 1948 Lanark)

Walter Smith was born in Lanark in 1948 and he grew up in Carmyle in the east end of Glasgow as a boyhood fan of Rangers. He trained as an electrician and gained employment at the South of Scotland Electricity Board before launching his football career in the 1960s with Junior League team Ashfield.

Smith signed as a defender with Dundee United in 1966, joining as a part-timer while working as an electrician. He was a good player who worked hard on his game. In September 1975 he moved to Dumbarton, but returned to United in 1977.

At the age of 29, a pelvic injury threatened his career and he was invited to join the Dundee United coaching staff by Jim McLean. His first team appearances were limited thereafter, but he remained a signed player and his final club match was in September 1980. In total, he made over 250 senior appearances, scoring three goals.

He developed his coaching skills, not only at Tannadice as assistant manager to Jim McLean, at a time when Dundee United were Scottish champions and European Cup semi-finalists, but also with the SFA.

In 1978 he was appointed coach of the Scotland Under 18 team, and helped Scotland to win the European Youth Championship in 1982. He became coach of the Under 21 team, and was Alex Ferguson's assistant manager during the World Cup in Mexico in 1986.

By then, Graeme Souness had invited him to become assistant manager at Rangers and he was instrumental in their success over the following years. When Souness left, Smith was appointed manager of the club in April 1991.

Seven successive league titles followed under Smith's tenure, including a domestic treble in 1993. He also won both the Scottish Cup and the Scottish League Cup three times each. In 1993, Smith took Rangers to within one match of the UEFA Champions League final. He signalled his intention to leave Rangers in October 1997 after a period of total domination of Scottish league football.

Rangers equalled Celtic's record of 9 successive championships in 1997 but were denied a record-breaking 10th success in 1998 as Rangers lost the title to Celtic and lost the Scottish Cup final to Hearts.

This marred a splendid managerial career but Smith left Ibrox in May with his reputation as one the most successful Scottish managers still intact. In his time as Rangers manager, Smith spent £45 million on an array of domestic and foreign stars.

Already hugely successful in Scotland, Smith accepted the offer to become manager of Everton in England in 1998. But financial constraints made it difficult for him to build a side that was capable of challenging for trophies. Walter parted company with Everton in March 2002.

In March 2004 Walter returned to football in a short spell as assistant manager to Sir Alex Ferguson at Manchester United until the end of season 2003/2004.

Smith beat off competition from Gordon Strachan to become manager of the Scotland national team and was appointed on 2 December 2004, succeeding Berti Vogts who had resigned in November.

Scotland have since seen an immediate turn around in fortune, although they we unable to gain enough points to qualify for the 2006 World Cup in the games he was in charge.

The weight circuit training exercises that we were asked to do, were not of the body building type, but more of the strength and toning side, keeping you nice and supple. The circuit was used for years and actually got named after the physio at the time, Andy Dickson. One lad named Gordon McLeod had a lot of talent and developed his physique quite quickly, having started to find fame at the ripe old age of 16.

To me this was an inspiration and it showed me that if you were good enough in the manager's eyes, then you were old enough, and you would get a chance to play in the first team no matter what age or size you were.

Dundee United, under the guidance of dedicated manager Jim McLean and Aberdeen under the guidance of Alex Ferguson, were now known at the time as the 'new firm'. They were challenging the 'old firm' of the two Glasgow clubs, Celtic and Rangers, for top status in Scottish football and were producing more terrific young players who were handed their debut at an early age.

Apart from the likes of Joe Miller and Paul Wright of Aberdeen, stars of the future such as David Winnie and Ian Cameron of St Mirren, Ian Durrant, Derek Ferguson and Robert Fleck of Rangers and Paul Shepard and Dougie Maguire of

Celtic, were just some of the youngsters who would soon be setting their sights on greater things. And with several other First and Second Division clubs in Scotland also producing some of their own young players as well, the prospects north of the border were now looking very rosy indeed.

As I started to develop into a burly 9 stone forward!! (Yes, the Andy Dickson circuit exercise routine was working), I was finally given my chance in Dundee United's first team. It was the time for me to show all and sundry what I could do.

On the 11 December 1985, I was named as a substitute against Neuchatel Xamax in the 2nd leg of a 3rd round UEFA Cup tie in Switzerland. We had won the 1st leg 2-1 and were confident of going through to the next round.

It proved to be a tight contest, and I can tell you, I was so nervous sitting on the bench that I managed to bang my head on the dug-out when Ian Redford scored a crucial away goal for us. I was suffering from blurred vision, but this didn't stop me from enjoying the moment, especially when the manager put me on the park for the last ten minutes. We were struggling at that point, 3-1 down on the night, 4-3 down on aggregate. Being out on the pitch was much better than having to watch the action from the touchline. It was so special for me to be involved in such a big occasion, despite our narrow defeat.

The line up on the 11th December 1985 was:
Thomson, Gough, Hegarty, Narey, Malpas, Milne, Beaumont, Kirkwood, Bannon, Redford, Coyne.
Substitues: Gallacher (for Milne), Clarke (for Coyne).
Attendance: 17,400.

Things were to go one step further when the manager spoke to me along with another young player, Paul Kinnaird, on the Thursday morning. I knew, deep down, that he was contemplating giving one of us our League debut on the Saturday, against Glasgow Rangers at

Ibrox Park. He told us that he was considering his decision but wanted to feel confident that both of us were ready for League football. I knew I was ready.

Both of us were kept waiting until an hour or so before the kick off. Would we both be in the starting line-up, or just one of us? It was tense, I can tell you that for nothing. But then the manager stepped forward and gave me the nod and boy, was I nervous.

With Ralph Milne an absentee, I was asked to wear the number 8 shirt. I played out wide on the right wing and although I can't remember a great deal about the game, I think I played reasonably well and helped the team earn a point from a 1-1 draw, which slotted us into 5th position in the table.

The full Dundee United line-up that day was:

Thomson (in goal); Malpas and Gough (full-backs); McLeod, Hegarty and Narey; Bannon, myself, Kirkwood, Redford and Dodds, with Holt on the bench. Davie Dodds netted our goal in front of almost 40,000 fans.

I never looked back after that. My next three games were all played in the space of seven days, either side of Christmas, against Aberdeen (won 2-1 at home), my boyhood heroes Celtic (also at home, won 1-0) and the local derby against Dundee (drew 0-0 at Tannadice).

On 4 January 1986, at long last, I scored my first senior goal – and it came against Celtic of all teams. Having beaten the Bhoys before the turn of the year, we were quietly confident of winning again, and we did, in style, running up a convincing 4-2 score-line over the champions-elect for that season.

It was a great feeling to get off the mark (in only my fifth senior outing) but it was a moment I will treasure for the rest of my life.

Still working hard and doing several bouts of extra training was the key to making progress, and indeed, keeping my place in the first team.

By now I was an established member of the side and it wasn't too long before I started to gain representative honours for my country.

I was capped by Scotland at both Under-18 and Under-21 levels and I was fortunate to link up with a striker with whom I formed a pretty useful partnership - Robert Fleck, later to play for Norwich City, Chelsea, Glasgow Rangers and others.

He was a snappy sort of player, as keen as mustard inside the penalty-area and a player who scored plenty of goals during a fine career.

I made good progress and finished the 1985-86 campaign with three goals to my

ENGLAND
v
SCOTLAND

21 · MAY · 1988 · KICK-OFF · 3.00 P.M.

THE ROUS CUP

THE FOOTBALL ASSOCIATION
125
ANNIVERSARY

OFFICIAL PROGRAMME £1.50

WEMBLEY
WHERE ELSE

credit (in 20 League games), helping Dundee United finish third in the table behind Celtic and Hearts.

Things were now developing faster than I had anticipated. I made over 40 appearances and scored 15 goals in League and Cup football during the 1986-87 season, but disappointingly I missed out on my first winner's medal when St Mirren defeated Dundee United 2-1 after extra-time in the Scottish Cup final in front of almost 52,000 spectators at Hampden Park. But things weren't all gloom and despair... for around this time I learned that I was on the brink of gaining my first full cap for my country.

However, that was to follow later rather than sooner!

The 1987-88 season saw us (Dundee United) again reach the final of the Scottish Cup. After knocking out Arbroath (7-0), Airdrieonians (2-0), Dundee (3-0 after 0-0 and 2-2 draws) and Aberdeen (1-0, following two more draws, 0-0 and 1-1), our final opponents were Celtic.

I knew it would be a tough game as the Bhoys were chasing the League and Cup double. We played well enough but in the end, despite me scoring what was to be one of the finest goals in my entire career, we again went down to a 2-1 defeat, Frank McAvennie netting both his side's goals in front of 74,000 fans at Hampden Park.

I was voted 'Man of the Match' in that final against Celtic and that to a certain degree, made the defeat a little more easier to accept, although a runner's-up medal wasn't what I expected. We could and should have won.

The Celtic team was:
McKnight; Morris, Rogan; Aitken, McCarthy, Whyte; Miller, McStay, McAvennie, Walker, Burns. Suns: Stark (for Whyte), McGhee (for Walker)

Twenty-four hours later, that cup disappointment became a thing of the past when I received a telephone call from Andy Roxburgh, the Scotland manager, who informed me that I had been chosen to represent my country. I was to play in the Rous Cup which involved matches against Columbia at Hampden Park and England at Wembley in this end-of-season tournament.

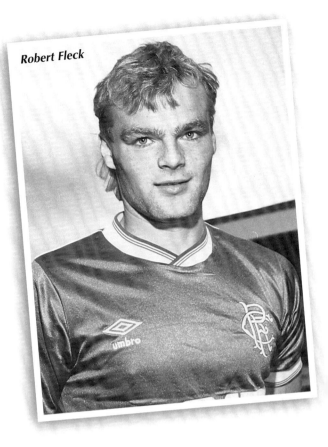

Robert Fleck

Obviously delighted, I made my debut against Columbia on the Wednesday evening, lining up alongside some of Scotland's top players, including Jim Leighton, Richard Gough, Steve Nicol, Alex McLeish, Roy Aitken, Paul McStay, Ally McCoist and Mo Johnston. It was a disappointing game, however, and in the end we had to settle for a 0-0 draw.

Four days later I got a fifteen-minute run out against the Auld Enemy, England, on the Saturday. I played against Arsenal's Kenny Sansom, one of the best full backs I have ever seen. A crowd of more than 70,000 saw us lose the contest 1-0, although if it hadn't been for a wonderful diving save by Peter Shilton, I would have earned us a draw.

That was just the start I had been hoping for, to get me going on a long and prosperous international career. I felt at this stage, that I was starting to follow in the footsteps of my footballing idols. Could I maintain my form? Stay clear of injuries and continue to improve. Time would tell.

chapter three

THE GODS OF SCOTTISH FOOTBALL

As a young kid I only heard stories of the likes of 'Gentleman' Jim Baxter, Billy Bremner and Dennis Law from my father and brothers when they were talking about football.

But when I realised that these international superstars were slowly but surely reaching the ends of their careers or had, in fact, finished, it still felt like I had watched them play.

My dad always talked about certain players he used to admire and watch whenever he could, or about those who played with and against him at Kilbirnie where, in his younger days, he appeared at junior and intermediate levels as a hard-tackling left back.

My two older brothers, Bernard and Tom, were always telling me that they used to take me along to see Celtic

play at least a couple of times a season, but those games just seemed to have passed me by without any trace – although they insisted that they were the ones who introduced me to watching the beautiful game of football.

My first actual memory of watching a senior professional football match was when my father took me to see my cousin, Stewart, play for Airdrieonians against Clydebank in the Glasgow Cup final at Firhill

That was, truthfully, the first match that really sticks out in my mind.

What I saw that night was to enthral me. As I sat back and watched the action, totally mesmerised while trying to take every thing in, I completely ignored as to how my cousin, Stewart, was playing.

I was so excited by the way some of the other players in the opposing side were playing, especially two young-looking lads, one occupying the centre of the park, the other playing out wide, that I didn't really notice my cousin. These two players really caught my eye and afterwards I learned that one was named Gerry O'Brien, a skilful midfielder with a great eye for a good pass and the other one was a youngster named Davie Cooper, a tricky winger.

Seeing these two lads play that night made me stand up with excitement and take notice.

They were brilliant at times. Cooper twisted and turned his opponents inside out, whipped over scores of inch-perfect crosses and fired in some cracking shots, while O'Brien passed with pin-point accuracy, showed an air of authority and judgment and dominated the play. Both players created chances aplenty for their fellow team-mates and certainly looked stars of the future.

Witnessing their performances that night got me excited and totally hooked on football. Stewart on the other hand came out of the dressing room and was a little dejected, not only had he finished on the losing side, but he really wanted to win the cup, so that he could show me his winner's medal after the match.

Unfortunately it was the runners up prize, but there always had to be a runner-up and although everyone wants to be a winner, taking part is all that matters deep down. I got to know this as time passed by.

Talking to Stewart afterwards, asking him loads of questions about football and footballers, I knew that I could go to bed at night dreaming about becoming a professional myself and then, in the morning, get my football out, go out into the garden, or nip around to the playing fields and try to copy some of the moves I had learned from the two lads I had just witnessed the night before.

On route to my primary school, St Eunam's, I had to walk past Kilbowie Park (formerly the home ground of Clydebank, and now a retail park).

Glancing across, I often imagined what it would be like to be a footballer, pulling on the green and white hoops and playing for Glasgow Celtic in front of 50,000 spectators. To score a winning goal in a Cup final was my dream.

But like all little boys, at that moment in time, it was just a big dream. After all, I was only about six or seven years old!!!! The more football matches I attended, the more hooked I got on the game and the more I wanted to become a football player.

As I grew a little older and my parents let me attend some local matches on my own, I used to walk up to my brother Bernard's house, which was only a goal-kick away from Kilbowie Park and hang around outside the ground trying to get a lift over the turnstile with anyone who would be willing to assist me… just so that I could get into the game for free and watch the match.

A lot of youngsters did that in my time. I was now starting to understand much

more about the game of football. I began to follow, check on and watch out for certain players and try to emulate everything that they did on the pitch.

I was not allowed to travel too far, following Clydebank was my only option apart from occasionally watching the game on the television, or failing that, if Bernard or Tom decided to take me along to Celtic Park.

That wasn't all that often.

Having by now witnessed a couple of players who I thought were fantastic, I was literally obsessed with my first real footballing idols, heroes if you like.

Clydebank were not renowned for having any superstars in the team, but they were a decent enough side who tried to pass the ball around rather than giving it the heave-to downfield or trying to brush past opponents by using physical strength.

Jim Gallagher in goal, was one of the best uncapped keepers of his day.

Jim Fallon and John McCormack were rocks at the back; Gerry O'Brien orchestrated things in midfield, spraying passes to all parts of the pitch with consummate ease, while the likes of Gerry Ronald and Davie Cooper were there to prise open the opposition defence with their dazzling skills and lay on crosses for striker Mick Larnach who certainly had a goalscoring touch.

Surely Clydebank could become a force, but unfortunately they only had a handful of full-time professionals. The rest of the players were only part-timers who trained twice a week and never really stood a chance when facing the top teams like Rangers, Celtic, Aberdeen and even Dundee United.

The club had to rely on eagle-eyed scouts, who scanned the country, seeking out young talent, stars of the future.

Several home grown players did exceptionally well and eventually were transferred for a healthy fee to one of the bigger clubs, and this really is how the minnows of the football world survived, even today.

Find a good 'un, sell him on, and start again. It's common practice in the game as far as the smaller clubs are concerned, always has been, always will be.

I know of several players who developed from schoolboy football.

I was one!!!!

But it is then down to the club they join. Someone, the coach mainly, is usually handed the responsibility of turning a promising youngster into a quality player. If he does, then that small, wee club will certainly survive and never fall into financial ruin!!!!

Clydebank had a little triangular red ash training pitch at the side of their ground and on a Tuesday and Thursday you were able to stand on a bridge and watch the players training. I did that quite often, just so I could catch a glimpse of the top players, if they were there of course.

Lots of the players are born with talent, but Davie Cooper was an exceptional talent. He seemed to stand out from all the rest and it wasn't too long before the big guns were contacting club Chairman Jack Steadman by telephone and letter, trying to entice their prize possession away from Clydebank football club.

Having been mesmerised by some of the things Davie could do with the ball, it had become inevitable that either Celtic or Rangers would buy him.

They had the money.

In the end it was Rangers who took the chance on him to my displeasure and at Ibrox Park he immediately started to produce the goods, showing everyone what he was capable of.

The skill just oozed out. He seemed to have a magic wand for a left foot… he could do anything with it. What glorious memories he gave the supporters and the Scottish public as well as being one of my first footballing idols.

Still, though, most of my attentions were at Celtic Park. I was always checking on their results, always reading match reports, seeing if they were doing well and if my all time idol, Kenny Dalglish, had scored a goal or two!

Being allowed to go to Celtic Park for the first time with my friends Joe O'Hanlon, Raymond Walsh and Paul Doohan, was an amazing experience for me.

I had played for the local boys team in the morning in Glasgow, and after the game we were all dropped off at my dad's pub from where we were able to walk a couple of miles down the road to Parkhead, along with all the other Bhoys' supporters. We would choose our place behind a barrier at aisle number seven or seventeen in the jungle (if there was room) and stand and watch the match, singing and cheering for the Bhoys.

Due to the fact that I was only able to attend certain home games, meant that I missed several big matches. But that made me more determined than ever to become a regular supporter, and as a result I saved up my pocket money, thus allowing me to see more games than normal.

While Kenny Dalglish was my favourite and I wanted to watch him more than any of the others, although having said that, it takes eleven players to make up a team, and I knew that there were some other quality players in the side anyway.

By the end of that season (May 1977) Dalglish was set to leave Celtic Park to enter the English Football League with Liverpool whose manager, Bill Shankly, a fellow Scot, would eventually pay £440,000 for his signature. King Kenny had scored 167 goals in 320 games for the Bhoys. What a player – and he would become an excellent manager in later years.

wall, posters of his boyhood Rangers idols! Dalglish was sent out to a Celtic nursery side, Cumbernauld United, and he also worked as an apprentice joiner. By the following year he had turned professional and was a regular member of a Celtic reserve team known as the Quality Street Gang.

It took Dalglish three years to establish himself in the first team. At that time Celtic were not only the best team in Scotland, they had become the first British team to win the European Cup after beating Inter Milan. Stein took a great interest in Dalglish, recognising his potentially outstanding talent. Eventually he gave him his chance in a benefit match.

The result was Celtic 7 Kilmarnock 2. Dalglish scored six of the Celtic goals!!!!

By 1972-73 Dalglish was Celtic's leading marksman with a seasonal tally of 41 goals in all competitions. Kenny's trademark of shielding the ball with his back to the goal had emerged.

Dalglish was made Celtic captain in 1975-

We need to encourage children nowadays to exercise themselves more. Football is as good as anything and the game will start to go in the right direction again. But they need some leadership and encouragement.

Kenny Dalglish

FACTFILE
KENNY DALGLISH
(born March 4, 1951, Dalmarnock, Glasgow.)

PLAYING CAREER
Kenny grew up supporting Rangers. Born in Dalmarnock in the East End of Glasgow, he was brought up in the docklands of Govan, just a stone's throw from Ibrox.

Kenny wanted to join his idols at Rangers, but the call never came. He had trials at Liverpool and West Ham, but to no avail. And so Kenny, the Protestant son of an engineer, found himself playing for Celtic, age-old fierce Old Firm rivals of Rangers.

His signing, on a provisional contract in July 1967, was not without amusement. Jock Stein, the legendary Celtic manager, had sent his assistant Sean Fallon to see Dalglish and his parents at their home.

Hearing that Fallon was at the door, Dalglish raced to his bedroom and frantically tore down the posters on his

76, but it was a miserable year. Stein was badly hurt in a car crash and missed most of the season. Celtic failed to win a trophy for the first time in 12 years.

Kenny had been a full Scotland international for six years, making his debut as a substitute in the 1-0 victory over Belgium in November 1971.

He went to the 1974 World Cup in West Germany. Scotland were eliminated at the group stage, even though they were undefeated. That spring of 1977 he had scored in Scotland's 2-1 victory over England at Wembley.

He moved to Liverpool in 1977, for a then-record £440,000 transfer fee, to replace Kevin Keegan, who left to play for Hamburg in Germany.

In his first season, Dalglish scored the winning goal in the European Cup final, against the Belgian side Club Brugge. He went on to become arguably the most influential member of the most successful club team in English football history, winning further League Championships and European Cups in a period stretching to the mid-1980s.

Kenny Dalglish in action for Celtic

MANAGERIAL CAREER

After the Heysel Stadium disaster in 1985, in the wake of the resignation of manager Joe Fagan, Dalglish became player-manager of Liverpool.

He coached them to their first-ever "double" — winning the League Championship (Dalglish actually scored the winner in a 1-0 victory over Chelsea to secure the title on the final day of the season) and FA Cup in the same season — in his first season, 1985-86. He continued as manager when he retired as a player, winning the League again in 1987/88 and 1989/90, and the FA Cup in 1988/89.

Dalglish was also in charge of the club at the time of the Hillsborough disaster, in the 1989 FA Cup semi-final against Nottingham Forest. He won many admirers for his exemplary dignity during this tragedy, and is still well-regarded by Liverpool supporters for this reason as much as for his on-field successes; ultimately, though, the trauma took its toll on his health, and he resigned as manager of Liverpool in February 1991.

Kenny Dalglish

Kenny went on to play in both the 1978 World Cup in Argentina, scoring against the Netherlands, and the 1982 World Cup in Spain, scoring against New Zealand. In total he played 102 times for Scotland (a national record) and scored 30 goals (also a national record, shared with Denis Law).

Kenny departed with his side still ranked as Champions, and as the dominating force of the English game for the past two decades.

Kenny returned to management in October 1991, with Blackburn Rovers, whom he led into the English Premiership in his first season. After winning the Premiership in 1995, Dalglish "moved upstairs" to become Director of Football at Blackburn..

In Spring 1997 he took control at a third top-flight English club, once again replacing the departing Kevin Keegan, this time as manager of Newcastle United.

In June 1999 he was appointed as Director of Football at Celtic, with his former Liverpool player John Barnes appointed as Head Coach.

PLAYING RECORD
- 1969-1977 Celtic 324 games, 167 goals
- 1977-1990 Liverpool 511 games, 172 goals (player-manager from 1985-1990)

HONOURS
- 4 Scottish Championships 1971/72, 1972/73, 1973/74, 1976/77
- 4 Scottish Cups 1971/72, 1973/74, 1974/75, 1976/77
- 1 Scottish League Cup 1974/75
- 7 English Championships 1978/79, 1979/80, 1981/82, 1982/83, 1983/84, 1985/86, 1987/88
- 1 FA Cup 1986 (as player/manager)
- 4 English League Cups 1980/81, 1981/82, 1982/83, 1983/84
- 3 European Cups 1977/78, 1980/81, 1983/1984
- 1 European Super Cup 1977

AWARDS
- PFA Players' Player of the Year 1983
- Football Writers' Association Player of the Year 1979, 1983
- Inaugural Inductee to the English Football Hall of Fame, 2002
- Scotland: 30 goals in 102 international caps (both national records)
- Member of the Scotland Football Hall of Fame
- Member of the FIFA 100
- Freedom of the City of Glasgow 1986.

MANAGERIAL RECORD
- Liverpool 1985-1991
- Blackburn Rovers 1991-1996
- Newcastle United 1997-1998
- Celtic (caretaker manager) Feb-May 2000
- English First Division Championship / Premiership 1985/86, 1987/88, 1989/90, 1994/95
- FA Cup 1986, 1989
- Promotion to the Premiership in 1991/92 (defeated Leicester City 1-0 in play-off)
- Scottish League Cup 2000

Now I could only follow my hero on the television and when he came back for the internationals at Hampden – if I could get a ticket.

Nevertheless, new heroes were to develop at Celtic Park for me to look out for in the near future. I would always seem to go there and idolise the forwards, although one or two others did actually catch my eye.

English-born Peter Latchford, ex-West Bromwich Albion, would feature prominently in goal. The bearded and much-liked Danny McGrain for instance was to become a fine full-back. Likewise Tommy Burns, later manager at Parkhead.

There were also the likes of George McCluskey, Frank McGarvey, David Provan, Murdo MacLeod, Brian McClair who went on to star for Manchester United, Roddie MacDonald, Dominic Sullivan, John Colquhoun and Frank McAvennie who later served West Ham United. Not all of them became household names with Celtic but they were pretty good players in their own right, and most

Scottish football is going through a similar phase like Northern Ireland did ten years ago.

David Moyes

Ally McCoist in action for Rangers

I've said, I had the privilege of playing with or against them at some stage during my own career. What an honour that was for me.

I remember the first time I played against my boyhood heroes, Celtic. I was starting on the right wing and in direct opposition to me was one of Scotland's best ever full backs, that man Danny McGrain!!!! For some strange reason he was switched to left back for this game.

I didn't know whether to bow, shake his hand or what, I was just full of admiration for this guy, but I had a job to do and I think I did a pretty good job. We beat Celtic and I managed to score my first ever professional goal.

When I went home to my parent's house that evening my friends all came around to congratulate me on my first ever goal, but then preceded to give me grief for beating our idols, Celtic.

Now that Kenny was in England it broadened my horizons, I could now watch other players whose names I recognised but hadn't even seen playing. Scottish players who were playing in England from a very young age, these lads had been taken down south with the English clubs scouting systems.

Alan Hansen, a cool centre back, who played at Partick Thistle before moving south to Liverpool. He should have represented Scotland more times than he did but the quality of centre-backs at the time was very good,

Graeme Souness, a tough solid competitor in midfield, Archie Gemmill, small balding man who will always be remembered for his goal against Holland and John Robertson, a stocky winger who could create something out of nothing with either foot, only to name a few, were legends in their own right, and to any young Scottish football fan like myself all you could do was look up to these guys and admire what they were doing for our country and hope one day you could do the same.

I was selected to travel with the Scotland

of them gained international recognition.

There was also Charlie Nicholas, flame-haired Gordon Strachan (who was to become Celtic's manager in 2005) and Ally McCoist whom I mentioned earlier, and of course, many others from several different clubs. I played with and against most of them, and believe you me, they were useful footballers.

Most of these lads were regarded as strikers, but not only could they score goals, some of them spectacular efforts at that, but they could also create chances for their colleagues with the ultimate piece of magic, whether it be trickery or just passing. Oh yes, these lads made it look simple.

Okay, some of them were signed from other clubs, but local ones like Charlie Nicholas came through the youth policy, and that meant a great deal to the supporters…a huge club producing its own players from local talent. That's great for the game.

Not only did I idolise these guys but as

under 18s to Finland and that's when I got a really good view of all my idols close up, sitting in the hotel foyer at Glasgow airport that evening minding my own business and just people watching, with the Liverpool players sitting together having a laugh in one corner, the Rangers and Celtic lads having a game of cards in the other and some just lazing around the bar area, to me this was amazing. Ok, I had played against a few of them by now but it was more the principle to meet Kenny Dalglish, Graeme Souness and all the others at first hand it was such a fantastic feeling.

FACTFILE
GRAEME SOUNESS
(Born Edinburgh, Scotland, 6 May 1953)

PLAYING CAREER

Graeme is one of the most committed players of his generation. He has won five League Championships, three European Cups and four League Cups during seven seasons at Anfield.

Graeme started his career as an apprentice at Tottenham Hotspur under Bill Nicholson but grew impatient at his lack of first team chances. Even though he was only a teenager, he famously told Bill Nicholson that he thought he was the best player at the club and should be in the first team!!!!

During the summer of 1972, the nineteen-year-old Souness played in the North American Soccer League for the Montreal Olympique. Graeme appeared in 10 of his team's 14 games, and was named to the league's first-team All-Star team for that season.

On his return to England, Graeme played just once for Spurs prior to a move to Middlesbrough F.C. in 1973 where he became a much-admired fearless midfield player who led a strong side over five seasons.

In 1974, he won his first cap for Scotland

in a 3-0 victory over East Germany.

After winning their first European Cup in 1977, Liverpool decided to seek reinforcements to defend their crown, as well as the League title they'd also just won. Three Scottish players in their 20s were all brought in by manager Bob Paisley over the next six months.

First arrived Alan Hansen, then Kenny Dalglish, and finally Souness, who cost £350,000 in January 1978.

These three would supply a superb spine in the side for seven glory-filled seasons.

Graeme settled in at Anfield but didn't feature in their European campaign until the semi-final He was instrumental in the final at Wembley when his pass set up Dalglish for the only goal of the game against FC Bruges.

That summer, Souness was selected by Ally McLeod for the Scotland squad for the World Cup in Argentina. He had only won six caps by this stage and injury robbed of him of a place in Scotland's first two group games against Peru and Iran.

With a defeat and a draw in his absence, his return was crucial as Scotland chased a victory by three goals or more in their final group match against the Netherlands but a 3-2 victory turned out not to be enough.

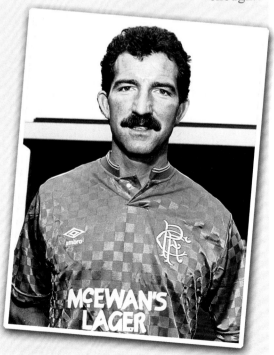

The following year Souness picked up his first League title medal as Liverpool coasted to victory and then retained it in 1980.

In 1981, Liverpool lost their League title to Aston Villa F.C. but won their first League Cup and their third European Cup with victory over Real Madrid. Graeme scored a hat-trick in the quarter-final against CSKA Sofia.

Bob Paisley's decision to give the captain's armband to Souness the following season helped to deliver two more trophies as Liverpool regained the League championship and the League Cup. Graeme went to the 1982 World Cup in Spain with Scotland and played in all three group games - versus New Zealand, Brazil and the USSR.

He scored his first international goal in the game against the USSR but again Scotland failed to progress.

The following year Liverpool again won the League championship and League Cup but Graeme relinquished his right as captain to lift the League Cup at Wembley after the 2-1 win over Manchester United F.C., instead insisting that Paisley collected the trophy in his retirement season.

In 1984, Souness lifted three trophies as Liverpool retained the League title and won the League Cup against fierce Merseyside rivals Everton F.C. A goalless first game was followed by a 1-0 win in the replay, with Souness hitting the only goal with a fabulous long-range strike. The European Cup was regained after a penalty shoot-out win over AS Roma before Souness, who had publicly expressed his wish to play abroad, was sold to Sampdoria for £650,000.

His Liverpool career ended after 358 appearances and 56 goals.

Graeme stayed in Italy for two seasons where his international career was coming to an end. Caretaker manager Alex Ferguson put Souness in his squad for the 1986 World Cup in Mexico and Souness played in two of the group games against Denmark and West Germany, both of which Scotland lost.

Graeme had scored the only goal of the game in a tremendous Scotland win over England just before that World Cup. Graeme made 54 appearances for Scotland scoring four goals.

MANAGERIAL CAREER

Graeme joined Rangers as player-manager for the 1987 season. Souness' final appearance as a player was at Ibrox in a 2-0 victory over Dunfermline in Rangers' last home game of the '89-'90 season. Graeme brought many Englishmen on the grounds, good players were the first requirement of a team wishing to succeed, irrespective of nationality.

Scottish players had long decamped south of the border to ply their trade but English players had rarely gone north until Souness arrived at Rangers.

It is probable that many English players were attracted to Rangers because the club could play in European competition, while all English clubs were banned from Europe between 1985 and 1990 following the Heysel Stadium disaster.

Rangers won four Scottish Premier League titles (1987, 1989, 1990, 1991) and four Scottish League Cups under Souness before he left to return to Liverpool in 1991 as manager after the resignation of Dalglish.

After an FA Cup defeat against Bristol City F.C. Graeme left Liverpool to manage Galatasaray in Turkey

Graeme returned to England to manage Southampton F.C. After he resigned, citing differences with chairman Rupert Lowe, he went back to Italy to become the coach at Torino Calcio before moving to Portugal to manage SL Benfica.

He then became manager of Blackburn Rovers F.C. earning promotion back to the Premiership in his first season and winning the League Cup in 2002. Souness left Blackburn in 2004 to become

> *Scottish players always had a big influence on English football. They were the main men in the bigger teams – but that's not been the case in recent years.*
>
> *Graeme Souness*

manager of Newcastle United F.C. and he remained in this job until February 2006.

CAREER HISTORY

PLAYER
- Tottenham Hotspur 1971-1973
- Montreal Olympique 1972
- Middlesbrough 1973-1977
- Liverpool 1977-1984
- Sampdoria 1984-1986

PLAYER-MANAGER
- Rangers 1986-1991

MANAGER
- Liverpool 1991-1994
- Galatasaray 1995-1996
- Southampton 1996-1997
- Torino Calcio 1997
- SL Benfica 1997-1999
- Blackburn Rovers 2000-2004
- Newcastle United 2004-2006

HONOURS AS PLAYER
Tottenham Hotspur
Winners
- 1968/69 FA Youth Cup

Middlesbrough FC
Winners
- 1973/74 Football League Second Division

Liverpool FC
Winners
- 1977/78 European Cup
- 1978/79 League Championship
- 1979/80 Charity Shield
- 1979/80 League Championship
- 1980/81 Charity Shield
- 1980/81 League Cup
- 1980/81 European Cup
- 1981/82 League Cup
- 1981/82 League Championship
- 1982/83 Charity Shield
- 1982/83 League Cup
- 1982/83 League Championship
- 1983/84 League Cup
- 1983/84 League Championship
- 1983/84 European Cup

Runner Up
- 1977/78 League Championship
- 1978/79 European Super Cup
- 1981/82 Intercontinental Cup
- 1983/84 Charity Shield

Sampdoria
Winners
- 1984/85 Italian Cup

Rangers
Winners
- 1986/87 Scottish League Cup
- 1986/87 Scottish Premier League
- 1987/88 Scottish League Cup

Runner Up
- 1988/89 Scottish Cup

HONOURS AS MANAGER
Rangers
Winners
- 1986/87 Scottish League Cup
- 1986/87 Scottish Premier League
- 1987/88 Scottish League Cup
- 1988/89 Scottish League Cup

Tartan Turmoil
the fall and rise of Scottish Football

- 1988/89 Scottish Premier League
- 1989/90 Scottish Premier League
- 1990/91 Scottish League Cup
- 1990/91 Scottish Premier League

Runner Up
- 1988/89 Scottish Cup
- 1989/90 Scottish League Cup

Liverpool
Winners
- 1991/92 FA Cup

Runner Up
- 1992/93 Charity Shield

Galatasaray
Winners
- 1995/96 Turkish Cup
- 1996/97 Turkish Super Cup

Benfica
Runner Up
- 1997/98 Portuguese League Championship

Blackburn Rovers
Winners
- 2001/02 League Cup

Runner Up
- 2000/01 Football League First Division

More idols followed as I got more involved at Dundee United, Hamish McAlpine, Richard Gough, Maurice Malpas, Paul Hegarty, David Narey, Eamon Bannon, Billy Kirkwood, Ralph Milne, Davie Dodds and Paul Sturrock, plus unsung guys like Derek Stark, John Holt and Frank Kopel.

Richard Gough

You looked up to all these lads. After all, I only went up to train in the school holidays so I only got to see them in the flesh for a few days. The respect you had for these lads was awesome.

These were great times and so exciting. Going back to school and being able to talk to your friends and compare which players you managed to speak to at your football club. Which ones you had a kick about with.

We compared our experiences on the International footballing superstars we played against in training sessions. Who you kicked or got kicked by and how they spoke to you.

Every time I went up to Dundee it felt very welcoming, from the staff working in the offices right the way through the club.

Watching World Cup matches brought in a flavour of the European talent. Guys like Paolo Rossi the Italian striker, Franco Baresi World class defender also from Italy, then there was Cruyff, Gullit and van Basten from Holland and the goal scoring machine of Gerd Muller from Germany.

chapter four
THE BEAUTIFUL GAME

Playing football in the street was an every day occurrence when I was a young boy…that is unless you could find a decent spare piece of grassland on which to have a proper game.

There weren't as many cars on the road in those days, so it was reasonably safe to play near the highway. We never had computers, gameboys or anything like that to keep us occupied. So apart from sitting in and watching TV for hours on end, there wasn't really much more to do other than go out and play football. That suited me down to the ground. But sometimes there weren't too many other boys who wanted to follow suit.

The weather didn't bother me. I would play in rain, sleet, snow, sunshine and mud. I just loved wearing my football strip, even a tracksuit or just some old clothes, to go out and have a kick-around.

I used to pick up my ball and off I would go, not a care in the world, hoping that I would find someone willing to join me. Most of the time a friend (or two) would turn up, one would go in goal and I would fire in shots at him as long as the light held good. Practice makes perfect they told me.

Whether there were twenty-two of you or just you and your mate, I always enjoyed playing football, kicking a ball around was great fun. I loved it.

Sometimes on a Sunday morning, when the playing season was over, my good friend Joe and I used to go to a primary school in Clydebank, called Our Holy Redeemers, and use their football pitch to play on for a couple of hours, shooting in at each other while taking it in turns to be goalie.

When it rained it meant extra washing for mum, but as long as it was not any of your good Sunday clothes for going out in, she would most likely forgive me.

Having only been able to play on the red blaze surface every week, it meant more holes in the tracksuit bottoms than anywhere else. In fact, I went through pairs of tracksuit pants like nobody's

business… and it was either a privilege or a cup final when you had the opportunity to play on a stretch of grass, even a marked out pitch.

Jim Mclean told me that his family always played football. "My oldest brothers' team won the All of Scottish intermediate shield and to him, it was 'fitba' 'fitba' 'fitba' all the time. There is no doubt whatsoever that the youngsters of today are getting much lazier in their approach to life in general. And those who want to play football are becoming far too casual in their approach. When I was a kid unless you could do the simple things in the game, control, kick and pass the ball, then you had no chance of making progress. No-one would even look at you. Now you can learn the skills of the game, become more efficient and make it enjoyable by joining coaching classes, recreation centres, youth clubs, academies etc."

Some of the dressing rooms they had were so bad it was like getting changed in the back of a van. There would be about eight changing rooms along a corridor, four on each side and they were like small square boxes with no room to swing a cat. If they were all occupied, it was pandemonium. So I began to copy what several of the lads were already doing, and that was to turn up, almost ready to play, with perhaps only my boots to put on.

Having a shower, well that was something else!

We had to suffer the consequences of a long standing, hopping round, freezing at times, in a long queue and normally when it was your turn to climb under the shower unit, the water was cold.

Oh yes, the facilities at some places, when I started my football career, were not the best I had ever seen – far from it. But we tossed everything aside and concentrated on playing the game we all loved so much.

Jim went on to say "There is absolutely no doubt at all that the facilities of today and the chances of making progress in the world of professional football, are far

> *The number of cars on the road today prevent street football. In my day all you needed was a ball. They canna play in the streets now and the park facilities are fewer. It's up to the councils to provide the facilities and to give the kids a little bit more respect. By giving the boys respect you will get them to play the game more.*
>
> *Kenny Dalglish*

more advanced than there were 20 years ago. In the good old days, we played on a small 50-yard pitch in a park. The goalmouth, even on a dry day, was muddy and bare because everyone loved goalmouth incidents. We practised all the time at crossing the ball, finishing and defending. There was no midfield really and the goalkeeper, bless him, was always in the thick of the action."

As I made slow, but sure, progress up the ladder towards becoming a professional footballer, I certainly expected the dressing rooms, the showers areas and such, to be better equipped. That was not the case, but we had to put up with what we had and honestly speaking, no-one moaned a great deal, especially if you had played well and won. When the weather was cold, and the frost got into your bones, it was then you needed a bit of hot water just to get the circulation going again in the fingers and toes. On many occasions, I simply couldn't undo my boot laces because my hands were frozen stiff!

On arriving at Tannadice, to start my apprenticeship with Dundee United, I found out from the coaches what facilities we had on offer. They were really good and at times it was a pleasure to use them, injured or not.

I moved up to Dundee (from Clydebank) and got fixed up with bed and breakfast accommodation with some of the other young apprentices.

It was a nice, big house on the Upper Constitution Road area of the town. It was summer time with June nearing its end, the weather was fantastic, and my digs were nice and cosy too. But it was all so different when the weather changed. I shared a room with a couple of lads, Colin Ainslie who came from Fife, and Billy Skinner from Inverness. We had a two-barr electric fire in our room and you could only light it when you filled the meter with lots of 5p pieces. As we never had a great deal of money to spend in those days, it was never lit all that often, although, when the biting wind blew into our room from the north, it was absolutely freezing! We tried all sorts of methods in an attempt to stop the draft from coming into the room, blocking the gaps in the windows with old newspapers, pushing carpets right up to the door, anything to make it a bit warmer. At night, when we went to our beds, we chose to go to sleep wearing our tracksuits, just to keep warm. We did try to heat the room up as best we could. When we were out at training though our landlady would come in, tidy up our room, take the newspaper out of the window frame, throw it all away and when we arrived back at the house, training over, it was back to a cold room. I can say that after a few months, we were all missing our home comforts.

We had to walk for half-an-hour to get to the stadium for our morning training session. We would leave the house at about 8.20am, just after a quick breakfast, to arrive at Tannadice shortly before 9am, as we had to finish all our jobs from the previous day before the senior professionals started arriving at around 9.30. We would get changed in the away dressing room with the second-year apprentices and the younger reserve players, while the first team players got changed in the home dressing room.

Come 9.45am, some of the apprentices were taken by mini-bus up to the NCR sportsfield in Camperdown (now a cinema complex) or to the local college of commerce's playing fields. Two sets of goals would be set up and a couple of football pitches suitably marked out, surprisingly, on a steep hill at the NCR so that the lads could go out and train. And woe betide you if you hadn't marked things out properly when the manager arrived. He used to go out and check everything meticulously, and if anything was wrong, you missed out on doing warm-up exercises as you would have to remark the pitch instead.

After the practice sessions were over, we would collect up the markers from the pitch, count them and put away the balls. We would then lock up the portable goals in a suitably provided container, and once

View from the corner of the Old Shed End at Tannadice

everything was spick and span and in efficient order, we would have to hang around, waiting for the mini-bus to return for a second trip after it had dropped the first team players back at the ground.

On arriving back at the club's ground, it was straight into the cleaning room to do the daily chores. There was a washing machine, a tumble dryer and a large table in the centre for rolling up the kit up after it had been laundered…and after all that had been completed, we headed off to the gymnasium for a general body and leg workout.

At Tannadice we had the privilege of having one of the first ever multi-exercise areas, which sat at the bottom end of a very dark gym. In fact, it looked more like an old-fashioned torture chamber than a gym. Of reasonable size, it comprised very small windows at roof height to let the light in, there were wall bars on both sides of the room and overall it was just about big enough for a small head-tennis court

to be placed in the middle. The machine had about a dozen or so different exercise stations on it, but the physio at the time was an old guy called Andy Dickson and he didn't really like anyone using the multi gym all that often. Instead he preferred us to do his circuit routine which he had set up many years previous.

Deep down, old Andy was a very nice chap – that is until it was time to do his circuit routine. He loved to see you struggle along while using all his knowledge on the physical side to make us stronger and help us grow into more efficient footballers.

He would never stop telling you about the 'Andy Dickson circuit' and how well it had served former top players like Doug Smith and Walter Smith before us. How the times have changed, back in the 1980s most football clubs would have only employed one physiotherapist and he had a lot of other things to do than just treating players. He would be in charge of all the medical kit and it was he and he alone, who was responsible for packing it all into hampers for the away games.

He was also in charge of packing up all the kit for away matches and sorting out the shirts, shorts, socks and tracksuits when we played at home. He was also the club's fitness coach and dietician, and besides taking the injured players for rehabilitation, he was regarded as the chief of the dressing room. Everything had to be place when old Andy was round – a great bloke.

Nowadays, football clubs have tended to share out a little bit of the responsibility to other individuals in order to cope with the modern day society. Several of the big-named clubs employ as many as three, four or even five physios/trainers, to look after each level of players (senior, second string and apprentices). Sometimes, there may be a couple employed at the academy where the younger kids are based, there could be two ready to treat the top stars and nine times out of ten there is always one in reserve.

In some cases, an established and qualified fitness coach is also brought in to concentrate solely on the physical aspect of the game. Whether it be getting the players warmed up before a training session or even a match, to taking the injured players for their rehabilitation or providing them with vital instructions on how to use the equipment properly when working in the gym. Some players require different information when working as an individual.

Some clubs employ a dietician who will ensure that each and every player looks after his own body. Basically he's there to see if you are eating and drinking the right food stuffs etc, and to decide what is the best food and drink to take and at what time.

For my lunch, I would have a pre-ordered sandwich from the local bakery accompanied by a cup of tea. In today's game, a player gets a small buffet, perhaps a selection of hot pastas, baked potatoes and salads from a buffet bar.

At Dundee United we had a snooker table in the executive box area and when the first team players had gone home after their morning training stint, the apprentices and reserves were often allowed to have a game on the green baize cloth. After that, it was back downstairs to continue working in the wash area prior to heading out in the afternoon for some individual coaching sessions on the nearby pitches. When time allowed, it was football, football and more football. What fun!!!!

The young players of the 1960s and '70s had even less facilities to work with. More often than not, after being signed up by a major professional club, they would invariably get farmed out to a junior side to harden them

Walter Smith (centre), Ally McCoist (right) and Tommy Burns (left) discuss tactics in the dugout

Tartan Tu...
the fall and rise of Scottish Footbal...

up for the years ahead.

Craig Brown recollects his early years: *"Things were a lot different in my playing days to what they are right now, totally different, in fact. I started in the same era as Alex Ferguson and Billy McNeill. We played in the same international schools team and youth sides together. We all eventually found League clubs and as part of our 'breaking in' and 'learning process' we were farmed out to a junior club."*

Therefore, for the first few years of their playing careers, they never really used the club's facilities on a daily basis – and this happened to a lot of the top stars.

Players like centre-half Billy McNeill, captain of Celtic when they won the European Cup in 1967, left Parkhead briefly to gain experience of competitive match play with Blantyre Vics; darting winger Jimmy Johnstone signed for Blantyre Celtic; hard-shooting full-back Tommy Gemmill and Craig Brown both had spells with Coltness United while the great Kenny Dalglish was farmed out to Cumbernauld United. It was more beneficial to these players to be involved in serious, competitive games at non-League level, playing against stronger and possibly fitter men each and every week, rather than competing in the reserves.

The facilities that these guys, and many more were used too, were relatively poor by today's standards, but they got on with the job to the best of their capabilities.

They reached the peak of their profession on pure hard work, self motivation and total dedication, which clearly emphasises why these players, and many more, are legends in Scottish football.

Lack of facilities didn't stop Kenny Dalglish becoming one of the best players our country has produced in recent years. *"We didn't have any! We had to use another school up the road. We played on the school pitch and sometimes the gym. We played in the streets and on a wee bit of grass at the top of the park. You relied on the school teachers who took the school teams. You gave 100%. We moved on to Glasgow schools. That was the first time we were introduced to a bit of organisation and coaching. At 16 years of age, you went maybe to a first division club. Invariably to get farmed out to the juniors. We ended up getting the "f!!k" kicked out of us. It certainly toughed you up. You know what I mean because of the injuries you picked up. That was the route for us."*

I would say that football in Scotland has never really suffered through the years because of the facilities provided. The players simply adapted to the environment, got on with what was on offer and what was available to them.

But why was it, that as the facilities got better, the players didn't improve as well as they would have liked?

Can you imagine the facilities that some of the greats like Denis Law and Jim Baxter had to use, football pitches with no grass, just mud, sometimes hard-packed and very bumpy, while in the gym, the use of medicine balls, boxing gloves, barbells were restricted to a very limited number, and in fact, this was virtually all they had to use apart from the normal match day football itself.

Yet many clubs, from all Divisions, continued to churn out top class footballers. How good would these players have been if the training facilities had been better? We shall never know.

In the winter months, normally between early November and late February, even early March, when at times most of the pitches were untrainable and even unplayable, players would go into the gym and do weight exercises or they take part in pre-arranged five-a-side matches on the hard surfaces of on a nearby car park. And at times, if a competitive match was scheduled to take place during mid-week, then it was basic running and jogging around the perimeter of the pitch, even trudging up and down the terraces top keep those leg muscles in trim.

Craig Brown told me a little story about all of this when he was at Rangers. He

Craig Brown

said: *"You never got the ball out, you just ran around the track. In fact, you used to put spikes on to train and you just ran and ran and ran. A wee player called Johnny Hubbard would run and run, then jump over the wall onto terracing.*

"The trainer was Dave Kinnear and he would shout out: "Johnny, where are you going?" Johnny would reply: "I'm up here for one of Sammy Baird's long passes.

There was always someone with a bit of humour inside them who would keep their spirits high, even on the lowest of days.

Although the players didn't like using the track, it was the only solution to the bad wintry conditions that plagued Scotland so often."

However, the pitches of today are so well looked after by the groundsmen, who regularly cut and trim the grass despite the weather conditions, continually flattening out and replacing the divots. All this is due to the upgraded technology in respect of the growing of grass and the amount of money that is now in the game. With that extra bit of cash, it's amazing, in today's world, what an array of new implements, seeds, top-soil and so forth can be acquired to get a football pitch in tip-top condition. With all this at hand, the groundsmen can obviously look after their patches far better than their predecessors.

Virtually every top club today, puts aside some extra cash in order to lay a new surface, a new pitch, just after the winter period has ended and when the grass is in a desperate state, looking rather forlorn. They have to budget for new turf, which a lot of the smaller clubs cannot afford to do.

It is now common practice for new stadiums to be built higher. All four corners of a ground are slowly but surely being filled in to allow for more seating. However, with the majority of the stands (four in some cases) fairly high at each ground, this doesn't seem to help the playing surface all that much, simply because it prevents the sun shining on the grass to provide the light it needs to help it grow, and also it restricts the wind from blowing in and drying out wet and damp surfaces. This is why we are now seeing more and more football pitches going bare long before the season ends. And also, one has to mention the drainage…this has to be in good, working order to stop the pitch from flooding after heavy downpours or thawing after snow and ice. And if the pitch is frozen, some clubs can switch on an under soil heating system – but some of the smaller organisations simply can't afford this sort of luxury - yet.

FACTFILE
CRAIG BROWN
(born July 1, 1940 in Lanarkshire)

Craig is a former Scottish professional football player and is currently employed in a director of football-style role at English club Fulham.

He played for Scottish schools, youth and junior International teams, before joining Rangers in 1959, aged just 19. He was unable to command a regular first team

place though, and moved to Dundee in 1962, where he won a League Championship medal. Craig stayed at Dundee for six years, before signing for Falkirk in 1967. He spent three successful seasons at Falkirk, before calling time on his playing career in 1971 after five operations on his knee.

He quickly shown a keen interest in being involved in the coaching side of football and he became assistant manager of Motherwell in 1974. He got his first managerial job as part-time manager of Clyde in 1977, where he spent ten seasons - winning the Second Division championship in 1982 - whilst also working as a primary school head teacher then a lecturer in primary education.

He returned to football full-time in 1986 when Scotland manager Andy Roxburgh appointed him as assistant manager. Brown was also in charge of Scotland's youth teams.

In 1989 he coached Scotland's Under-16s to the final of the world championship and three years later coached the Under-21s to the semi-finals of the UEFA championship.

Craig was appointed as manager of Scotland in December 1993, having been caretaker manager, with responsibility for games against Italy and Malta, since Andy Roxburgh's resignation in November.

Following the failure of Roxburgh's side to go to the World Cup 1994, however, Brown soon made up for this by taking Scotland to Euro 96. He also took Scotland to France 98, but resigned in 2001 having failed to take Scotland to Euro 2000 and World Cup 2002.

Under Craig, Scotland beat England in the last ever Euro Championship qualifier at Wembley in 2000 by one goal to nil.

He then had a spell in club management when he was appointed as manager of Preston North End in 2002 but left in August 29, 2004.

The players of today are looked after very well indeed, simply because they can go to the indoor arena attached to the training ground and have a serious work out, or failing that, there is also the added bonus of having that under soil heating within the stadium compounds.

nice, smart local environment again. I'm sure it would help immensely."

Craig went on to say: *"There is not one indoor full size soccer pitch in Scotland, or even in the U.K. You can't say The Millennium*

National Indoor Arena, Birmingham

Craig Brown and I once had a chat about the facilities in Scotland and top of the list was the possibility of an indoor complex which could take a full size football pitch.

He pointed out to me by saying: *"In his last year at school there were 28 Norwegian footballers playing in the SPL. While there's only around six Scottish lads. To think that Norway has a smaller population than Scotland, I don't know. But I do believe that by using extra facilities - going out to play in the street as against using other suitable alternative playing areas, like park pitches, school playing fields - would certainly create a*

Stadium in Cardiff can be used by everyone. There are three in Moscow and about a dozen in Norway, three in the one city."

He then recalled a match he saw in Moscow between Spartak and Skonto Riga which took place in an indoor arena. He said: "The goalkeeper can kick the ball as high as he likes and it may just touch the netting under the roof of the stadium which had to be fixed about 30 metres above the pitch itself. FIFA may now have relaxed the ruling to 20 metres but when the ball hit the net it would come back into play. No stopping for a bounce up."

Rangers' Ian Ferguson takes on Dino Baggio of Parma

Alex Ferguson in Pre-Season managing Aberdeen

He then proceeded to say: "Every time you go and see a reserve match these days, the pitches are often in a really poor state, but if you had a quality indoor arena, it could make all the difference. The person who builds the first one with around 4,000 seats, could possibly make a fortune, simply because if it is erected in the right place, central to a lot of clubs, you could possibly have a whole load of reserve games played on it on a daily basis".

In today's society surely we should have a

lot more and, indeed, far better facilities to use during the winter seasons!

When Sir Alex Ferguson was in charge at Aberdeen in the early 1980s, they used to have several youth teams; they would have teams in Glasgow, Edinburgh and Aberdeen. Now out of these teams you may get one or two good players, so he decided, for financial reasons, to pick only the best footballers out of these three or four teams they were running and create one useful side.

Unfortunately, in this case, some good players slipped through the Dons' net, as this was to be with Ian Ferguson who went on to become a £1 million player with Rangers.

The facilities have changed slightly over the course of time, and so has the amount of top quality talent. When I was 13 years of age and on a schoolboy contract, I was only involved with Dundee United at youth team level when the club competed in the professional FA Youth Cup tournament or participated in a young lads' trial game which was normally staged in the school holidays. Nowadays, there is a Centre of Excellence attached to most clubs, and from a very young age, kids can hopefully make steady progress into various football academies up and down the country.

Nowadays, at a very early age, young players and their parents get offered lots of money to go to the best clubs, some receive up to six-figure fees and that is seen to be a good investment by a lot of the big named clubs, simply because if the lad in question doesn't make it with their top team, they can readily sell him on to another club for a substantial fee and at the same time recoup the money they paid him initially, plus a little extra on the side.

All profits are put back into the academies' set up and the whole process starts all over again. It makes sense, doesn't it?

Clubs get a grant of about £138,000 from the FA in England for running a Centre of Excellence. The cost is far higher in most cases. Academies are far more expensive even than that.

The players at an academy are now full time, provided with meals, living accommodation and paid a wage. It costs the same amount of money for a young lad to have a scan for an injury as it would for one of the club's top players.

So, is having an academy an answer to our needs in Scotland to produce Internationals of the future?

Is it an expensive tool or is there a better way to spend what money is available?

Do clubs get value for money?

I think the answer to each of these three questions is probably yes.

Today, there is a lot of talk in Europe about teams having an artificial grass surface on which to play their home games. Dunfermline Athletic are already trying it out, although their surface is rather poor…but could this be the way forward?

Oldham Athletic, Luton Town, Queens Park Rangers and Preston North End all tried this down in England in the 1980s and '90s and the players who performed on these sort of surfaces didn't like it at all, some of them complaining of burns to the legs, elbows and shoulders, caused by skidding or falling on the pitch itself. Although today's technology is a lot more advanced, with the new artificial grass being introduced at regular intervals, I think you may get the same problems.

The only plus side, I feel, would be if every club had an artificial grass pitch. This would then give every player an even surface on which to perform. But that will never happen, certainly not in the U.K.

The footballing bodies of UEFA and FIFA are working on new surfaces of the plastic variety, trying hard to get it to play just like grass.

Sepp Blatter said something like this: "If they can put a man on the moon in this day and age then surely they can simulate grass artificially."

There are a lot of people out there who will immediately disagree with this suggestion, especially the players whose careers could well be cut short due to the amount of injuries they would receive from all the continuous pounding of the ankle, knee and hip joints they would suffer, week in, week out, on the harder surfaces. It was said that a lot of players in England finished their careers early because of the artificial surface. But times change and "plastic grass" may not be that far away or a bad thing. You only have to look at the state of pitches at the top stadiums like Old Trafford or Chelsea!

The state of Scottish football facilities of today, in my opinion, is shocking. How can youngsters get enjoyment out of playing football on a small, indoor pitch.

Craig Brown

chapter five
GRASS ROOTS

When I was young lad all you needed to play a game of football was four jumpers and a ball.

I think back to those early days of playing football in the street as a kid, these were the main pieces of equipment you had if you were lucky.

My parents couldn't afford to buy me golf clubs, tennis rackets or spend hundreds of pounds on computers and gameboys. So for them, to buy me a football was seen as the cheaper investment and it would keep me out of a lot of mischief.

When setting out in the world of football, no one ever looks back at the earlier side of their game; they all tend to forget how or where they first got started.

It would commence, of course, with kicking anything from an empty can to a tennis ball, from a rolled up piece of paper or cardboard, secured by a few elastic bands, to a knob off an old door, all the way to using a proper blown-up full-size football. Oh yes, we don't realise how much times have changed.

I don't think there are too many kids of today who are inclined to play football. I used to play twenty four hours a day and seven days a week, plus another two hours of football combined into a P.E. lesson. An odd week playing the game, even kicking a ball around for fun, is not going to make you into the next Ally McCoist, Denis Law or Davie Cooper. It takes a lot of long hard hours of practice to get you that far.

With the change in the environment, parents don't want to let their kids out of sight for too long these days. With such a wide choices of things to do indoors, it seems to be the safest option to allow children to pop down to the local youth club, the church hall, even the community centre, where in most cases they are under supervision.

In my younger days, I was totally blinkered by football. No matter what the weather was like, rain or shine, I simply ate, drank and slept football!!!

My mother once said to me that from the day I was conceived I had football in my genes.

So, one day, I tried to look inside the pocket of my pair of Levis to see if I could find it!!!

All I ever wanted was a football strip; it didn't matter which team it represented, and with it a ball. It was then up to me to practice.

You don't have to have a family history in football but like all young kids, I had a dream!!!

I dreamt of becoming a football player, and to make that dream come true I would have been already working hard on my football skills without even realising it. As soon as I got my first football and kicked it for the first time, that was it for me. I was hooked. I had taken that vital first step, but it was never that easy, believe you me.

There would still be a lot of hard work and dedication ahead as well as a little but of luck.

My friends and I would always carry a ball wherever we went. We would take off some part of our clothing, usually a jumper, and lay it on the ground before starting to have a general kick around. Occasionally, if we were able to occupy the grass area, I recall using a couple of large wooden sticks for the goalposts.

We would then choose the two oldest people to be captains, who would then in turn, select players for each team. When that was done it was straight into a match. It was sometimes serious with free kicks, throw-ins and corners being awarded, but not always the norm, as we were still learning the rules of the game as we went along.

I frequently went along to a local school which had real fixed metal goalposts with a cross bar on, situated on a red ash surface. I played there for hours, just shooting into and at the goal. If one of my friends was there, then one of us would do all the shooting and the other would be the goalkeeper or the gofer, just collecting the ball for the other person as it whizzed between the posts, over the bar or went wide.

Games like this used to be played all the time, especially by the larger families who had two or three boys, keen to get involved in football.

I remember my old Dundee United manager Jim McLean once telling me

"Practice makes perfect. The more you practice the better you become." I will never forget that and, in fact, I have used those same words elsewhere in this book. It's absolutely right – not only for future footballers, but for all young, up and coming sports-minded men and women.

McLean went on,

"And we always had a ball to play with. Nowadays, it's a lot different.

Teenagers are more interested in computers and such likes. They choose to sit on their arses and tap away on a keyboard facing a screen, or guiding a joystick from side to side as the hero attacks the villains in a TV game.

Others buy magazines, puzzle books and mobile phones with loads of gadgets on them.

On average, only two out of ten youngsters are interested in football. And this has to be improved. Get more youngsters involved in the game. Arrange for school trips to watch matches, take boys to training sessions, get coaches into schools to give talks, get players to do the same.

It will work in the end, believe me.

If say two or three youngsters (out of 20) think they might just enjoy playing football, arrange a few lessons, perhaps privately, get them kicking a ball around.

The famous golfer, Gary Player, once said: "The more you practice the luckier you get" and there is no doubt at all that the kids of today need to practice more. Don't just let them have a kick-around willy-nilly.

Get an organised game arranged; ask for those interested to turn up with their boots, and if this can happen, occasionally why not ask a senior professional from the local club to pop along and show his face at the game. It will all help in the long run.

They say practice makes perfect and that's absolutely right."

It was not just in my time, it was done by better players years before me. Jim McLean's brother Tommy (of Glasgow Rangers fame) used to do something very similar. He frequently walked to a nearby piece of land and practised chipping and crossing the ball for his friend. He would shoot, trying to use both feet, bend it with the inside or outside of his foot, just to enhance his skills.

He would practice with the ball, sometimes on his own, for a couple of hours after school every day while his friend, bless him, would just run around collecting the ball for him. That's what made Tommy one of the best crossers of the ball in his era.

Playing on red ash surfaces I would probably say improves your touch. With the ball bobbling around all the time, you had to concentrate more than you would have done on a flat surface, even on a grass pitch. And if you were a defender,

...This needs to be looked at by bodies from the Scotland Education sector – and their priority must be about getting extra money for the teachers who, I'm sure, would give up their spare time on a Saturday once they know they would be paid for their efforts in coaching the young footballers of the future.

David Moyes

Everton Manager David Moyes, collects a Manager of the Month award

you never attempted a sliding tackle, or else! You always tried to stay on your feet and I think that's why, in years gone by, Scotland had some of the best passers of the ball in the game. They also had some of the best defenders and also some of the best goalscorers too.

Over the last two or three decades, the quality and quantity of school P.E. and sporting activities in general, has fallen. Among the contributing factors is the declining willingness of teachers to organise team games outside school hours.

School football had a major affect on the way my football career started.

At school, when P.E. was in the agenda, we were given quite a choice. We could play table tennis, badminton, hockey or football, to name a few, indoors and outdoors. But with it being a predominantly footballing school, most of the boys wanted to play football and sometimes the teachers would join in the action. The rest of the time, it was down to the boys to organise a game between themselves. It worked fine.

It was all down to our P.E. teacher, Mr Speirs. It was a Friday afternoon, we had a game of football during our P.E. lesson and both of the P.E. teachers, Mr Speirs and his colleague, Mr McCluskey, joined in the action.

After dribbling rings around both of them, Mr Speirs took me aside and said that he hadn't seen me playing football for the school team.

"Why was that" he said. "I haven't been selected" I replied.

At that point, he threatened to stop me playing for my Sunday side, Duntocher Boys, if I didn't turn out for the school football team, saying that the school needed players like me. So after a bit of gentle persuasion, I reluctantly went on to play and captain my school football team, but I still played for Duntocher Boys as well!!!

The one teacher who had dedicated his time to the school football team was a

gentleman called Dave McCulloch. He took the engineering, science and woodwork classes. He was a quiet man with longish dark hair and a rough bearded look (I think he wanted to be George Best). Mr McCulloch gave up a lot of his spare time and put in a great deal of effort by taking the team around the country to compete in football matches against other schools.

He did it all on his own, with some occasional help from any parent that happened to be there watching his son. And he didn't even get an extra £1 in his wage packet for the effort he put in. That was total dedication for you, doing so much for the sport he loved.

He chauffeured us around, looked after us, put up a team list to tell us who was in the squad and who we would be playing against that weekend. And surprisingly, to this day, I can't ever remember him actually trying to coach football.

He just picked eleven players, put them into a position he thought best, organised us and let us get on with the game. I must say though the team we had was a very successful one, and we won quite a few trophies.

With so many complaining that youngsters do not get much of a chance these days, it is good to hear that the Bank of Scotland plan to plough £1.5 million into grass roots football in Scotland. The funding is targeted at 140,000 young people at secondary school level to allow them to play and develop their football skills through training, development and organised competitions.

It just seems nowadays that certain schoolteachers don't have enough time on their hands to get involved in any sort of sport. Is this because of their heavy workload?

Selling off of so many playing fields nationwide probably contributes to the fact that there are so few sports days on the school calendar?

With the changes in the environment plus strict health and safety rules, which have to be obeyed, teachers don't need the hassle anymore. So if they all choose to give up the responsibility of looking after a team, whether it be on a football or rugby pitch, on a cricket square, in the swimming pool or out on the running track, there will soon be no sport whatsoever on the school timetable.

There is also the added bug-bear of having to gain an official coaching licence to coach and supervise youngsters. Teachers and sports masters feel totally inadequate, and unable to run the football teams because of their lack of a licence.

Having said that, there are several courses for the teachers to go on and ultimately achieve the required licence. But it seems, to me that they are happy to leave the football to the local Sunday team organisers and to the professionals. As a result, at most schools and boys' clubs all over the country the coaching standards have seriously declined over the last few years.

Perhaps surprisingly, in some respects, many talented youngsters still tend to appear when least expected, recommended to a senior club scout, coach or manager, by their respective P.E. teacher or sports supervisor or leader, Wayne Rooney, Joe Cole, Steve Gerrard, David Beckham and Michael Owen being amongst them.

By pushing the coaching when the kids are so young we are stereotyping the individual. We are maybe taking the enjoyment out of the game!!!

But I don't think so.

Helping the kids develop more of their ball skills, and teaching them more of the game's technical side will make them more aware of what the sport is all about, and at the same time appreciate the fact that working on the general fitness routine would come when the lad starts to play in competitive matches and come face to face with stronger, bigger, older and more experienced opponents.

Three games at the weekend and one or

two at night during the summer months was the amount of football I played to get myself started. That was quite a hectic programme.

Duntocher Boys Club was a very useful village outfit, with most of the players ranging from Under 11 to Under 16, although eventually an Under 18 side was formed. And I believe there were younger teams as well.

At least six or seven of the boys, aged between 13 and 16, became attached to professional clubs because of the club's success. So our success rate in producing good footballers was very high. Sadly, though, only one or two of them went on to become full-time professionals.

In the past, most of the professional clubs

At 13 years of age a youngster can suddenly develop in double-quick time. Unfortunately some of them don't make it.

Jim McLean

had their own type of youth set up and several in the 1980s used to be associated with several boys teams around the country. The professional club would have first choice on all of their players, therefore running a youth set up similar to today's academies in England.

This seemed to be costing the various clubs quite a lot of money. As a result many of them decided to change the format and run just one team, instead of two or three. They took the best players out of all the sides, rather than having several reasonable ones to choose from, thus ending up with a decent sized squad.

Ex-Scotland manager Craig Brown told me that;

"several of the younger players these days, especially those registered with the bigger clubs, Celtic, Rangers, Aberdeen,

are loaned out to a junior team. This was the case when I was starting off... some went to Lewis United. And I recall Aberdeen sending Willie Miller off to a Highland League side to gain experience.

Some years later, when 'Fergie' became manager of Aberdeen, he was associated with youth teams all over the west coast. He also had a couple on the go in Aberdeen and one in Edinburgh.

In the end, he knocked them all on the head, saying: "It was a waste of money running these type of teams, especially when there is perhaps only one boy, sometimes two, who makes the grade.

The SFA recently appointed a new chief executive and Alex McLeish (then Rangers' manager) was prepared to go to one of the SFA meetings and tell them to forget the Under-19 set up...it's not working.

He thought it best to take the best players out of the Under-19 team and farm them out to intermediate League clubs. That's a better way to entice a young player forward.

When I played in junior football - it's similar to being a semi-professional in England - Billy McNeill was quickly pushed out to Blantyre Vics, Jimmy Johnstone to Blantyre Celtic and myself and Tommy Gemmell to Coltness United in Lanarkshire. We played with and against men much older than us; we were 16 or 17 years of age, our opponents were 18, 19 and sometimes 20. Billy McNeill finally established himself with Celtic when he was 19 and then he played only in the reserves.

Today, you get guys who are winning the European Cup, the UEFA Cup, Premier League titles and so forth as teenagers. That's how the game has changed over the years.

I recall Alex Ferguson phoning me one day when I was at Clyde. He told me that he was doing away with the Aberdeen boys' club in East Kilbride and offered me three

Jimmy Johnson

young players, one was Ian Ferguson, later to become a £1m footballer. Well, I would have never though that Alex would have got rid of such a talented player, but he did.

If I identified or found one good player in Glasgow, or one from each age group (Under-16, Under-17 whatever) I would have sent them to Pollock Juniors, Petershill or Shettleston."

Dundee United attempted to get two or three players from different teams in an effort to formulate a decent squad for their youth team, and they also included a handful of trialists as well.

Most top clubs are now starting with the kids as young as nine, some even younger, but taking a gamble with someone that age is a risky business. The question you ask yourself is, will he be good enough when he is older?

Former Scotland boss Craig Brown has a firm view on this,

"When I was a young lad, eager to play football where and when I possibly could, I joined my local team and enjoyed kicking a ball around as best I could, until, hopefully, one day you got noticed by someone representing a major club."

The laws of the game stated at that time, that no professional club could sign a young lad until he had reached his 13th birthday. Kid's up to the age of 11 should, in my mind, enjoy football and develop their own talent without the rigours of coaching. It seems to me that a boy, aged between 11 and 14, tends to retain things easily and certain aspects of a specific subject sticks in his mind far better.

By the time he reaches the age of 15, he should know the difference between right and wrong. Mid-teens are when he matures and becomes more intelligent (hopefully) but also a time when other interests are around and there will be the temptation to experiment with alcohol, girls and unfortunately drugs. But if he wants to succeed in football, he will have to take serious advice on these distractions.

Andy Roxburgh

The Scottish Football Association is trying to attract more youngsters to its soccer schools in order to help them learn about the beautiful game. There are coaching courses in nearly every region of Scotland right now, so one feels that there must be one or two budding stars of the future out there waiting to be snapped up.

When Andy Roxburgh introduced all of this, it proved to be a terrific idea, the best thing that had happened in the game for many a year. He seemed to be way ahead of his time on the coaching front. His thoughts were to get top international players interested in coaching, so that the youngsters would follow suit. But first and foremost he had to get the help of some of Scotland's finest coaches to make it work.

Enter Alex Ferguson and Jim McLean, legendary football coaches and respected by all throughout the Scottish game. They were the men who would eventually help

In my opinion, beyond any shadow of a doubt, the youngsters of today are not hungry enough. In days gone by, there always used to be well-known boxers and many footballers from Glasgow

Jim McLean

Tartan Turmoil
the fall and rise of Scottish Football

Andy Roxburgh fulfil his target and entice the professional football player to step up and take his coaching badge.

Alex Ferguson with a young fan at the 1999 FA Cup Final

FACTFILE
SIR ALEX FERGUSON
(born 31 December 1941 in Govan, Glasgow)

PLAYING CAREER
He began as an amateur at Queen's Park, making his debut at 16 as a striker. Although he scored 15 goals in his 31 games for Queen's Park, he could not command a regular place in the side and moved to St Johnstone in 1960.

He continued to score regularly at St Johnstone but was unable to command a regular place. His chance came against Rangers where he scored a hat trick in a surprise victory. Alex signed for Dunfermline the following summer (1964.)

In the 1964-65 season, Dunfermline were strong challengers for the Scottish League and reached the Scottish Cup Final.

In 1967, he joined Rangers for £65,000, then a record fee for a transfer between two Scottish clubs. The following October, Nottingham Forest wanted to sign Ferguson, but his wife was not keen on moving to England at that time so he went to Falkirk instead.

He was promoted to player-coach there, but when John Prentice became manager he moved to Ayr United, where he finished his playing career.

EARLY MANAGERIAL CAREER
East Stirlingshire
In June 1974, Ferguson was appointed manager of East Stirlingshire, at the comparatively young age of 32. It was a part-time job that paid £40 per week, and the club didn't have a single goalkeeper at the time. He immediately gained a reputation as a disciplinarian, with one of

his players later saying he had "never been afraid of anyone before Ferguson arrived". His players admired his tactical decisions, however, and the club's results improved considerably.

The following October, Ferguson was invited to manage St Mirren. Although they were below East Stirlingshire in the league, they were a bigger club and although Ferguson felt a degree of loyalty towards East Stirlingshire, he decided to join St Mirren after taking advice from Jock Stein.

St Mirren
Ferguson was manager of St Mirren from 1974-1978. Despite having to look after the team with a small budget, he was able to achieve promotion for the side to the Scottish First division in 1977. However, due to a dispute with the club's chairman, he moved on.

Managing Aberdeen
Ferguson joined Aberdeen as manager in June 1978. Although Aberdeen was one of Scotland's major clubs, they had not won the league since 1955.

The team had been playing well, however, and had not lost a league match since the previous December, having finished second in the league the previous season. Ferguson had now been a manager for four years, but was still not much older than some of the players. The season saw Aberdeen reach the semi-final of the Scottish F.A. Cup and the final of the League cup.

The following December (1979), they lost the league cup final to Dundee United after a replay. Aberdeen started the following season poorly but their form improved dramatically in the new year and they won the Scottish league that season with a 5-0 win on the final day.

It was the first time in fifteen years that the league had not been won by either Rangers or Celtic. The team continued their success with a Scottish Cup win in 1982. Ferguson led Aberdeen to even greater success the following season (1982-83). They had qualified for the European Cup Winners' Cup as a result of winning the Scottish Cup the previous season, and impressively knocked out Bayern Munich, who had beaten Tottenham Hotspur 4–1 in the previous round.

According to Willie Miller, this gave them the confidence to believe that they could go on to win the competition, which they did, with a 2–1 victory over Real Madrid in the final on 11 May 1983.

Aberdeen became only the third Scottish team to win a European trophy.

Aberdeen also performed well in the league that season, and retained the Scottish Cup with a 1–0 victory over Ranger.

After a poor start to the 1983-84 season, Aberdeen's form improved and the team won the Scottish league and retained the Scottish Cup. Aberdeen retained their league title in the 1984-85 season, but had a disappointing season in 1985-86, finishing fourth in the league, although they did win both domestic cups. Ferguson had been appointed to the club's board of directors early in 1986, but that April he told Dick Donald, their chairman, that he intended to leave that summer.

After the death of Jock Stein he had also taken on the role of Scotland manager in preparation for the 1986 World Cup, appointing Archie Knox as his co-manager at Aberdeen during this time.

There had been speculation that he would take over from Ron Atkinson at Manchester United, who had been struggling badly that season after a good start. Although Ferguson remained at the club over the summer, he did eventually join Manchester United when Atkinson left the club in November 1986.

Managing Manchester United
Record at United

- League games: 707
- Charity/Community Shield: 11
- League Cup: 65
- FA Cup: 78
- Euro Cup/Champions League: 116
- Cup Winners Cup: 13
- UEFA Cup: 4
- Super Cup: 2

Alex Ferguson in his managerial days at Aberdeen

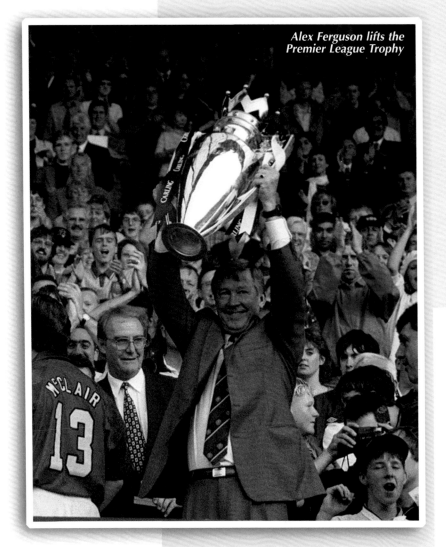

Alex Ferguson lifts the Premier League Trophy

- World Club Championship: 3

- Toyota Cup: 1

- FA Premiership: (8) 1992/93, 1993/94, 1995/96, 1996/97, 1998/99, 1999/00, 2000/01, 2002/03

- Runners up: (3) 1991/92, 1994/95, 1997/98

- FA Cup :(5) 1989/90, 1993/94, 1995/96, 1998/99, 2003/04

- Finalists: (2) 1994/95, 2004/05

- League Cup: (2) 1991/92, 2005/06

- Finalists: (3) 1990/91, 1993/94, 2002/03

- FA Charity/Community Shield (5): 1993, 1994, 1996, 1997, 2003

- Finalists: (5) 1998, 1999, 2000, 2001, 2004

- Shared :(1) 1990

European competition

- UEFA Champions League :(1) 1998/1999

- European Cup Winners Cup :(2) 1982/83*, 1990/91

- Intercontinental Cup :(1) 1999 (aka Toyota Cup since 1980)

- UEFA Supercup: (1) 1983/84*, 1991/92

- Finalists: (1) 1999/00

Total trophies won: 26

If Alex Ferguson and Jim McLean had to do it, then the players knew that they would have to follow suit and there was the big attraction for the young up-and-coming footballer…he could possibly be the one who would be coached by an idol.

Football coaching courses have been around for many generations. My first experience of such a course was at a college in Glasgow. And I got to go there after winning a soccer skills competition at school. My prize was to be coached by a top professional footballer, and when I turned up on the first day, there were one or two players there too. I was placed into a group run by a coach from Morton. I remember receiving a T-shirt and some other goodies, as well as a certificate for attending the weekly course.

Grass roots football coaching is widely available but with today's environment parents are happier when they can see what their child is up to, rather than placing him in the hands of someone else, some one strange to the family. It's a way of life.

So unfortunately, unless the parent is prepared to travel every where with his or her child, I think Scottish football could be losing the budding footballer to the ever growing computer whiz kid. Hopefully not, but we shall see.

Tartan Turmoil
the fall and rise of Scottish Football

*Scotland vs England
School Boys*

chapter six

GROWTH OF THE ACADEMIES

We all talk about growing home talent and developing the game at international level, but are the Scottish Football Association and its associated clubs willing to do something about it? And is there enough being done to help the new generation of players?

Yes, we are getting quite a few young players coming through the ranks, but not at the rate one would be hoping for and which would see several top-line English clubs come knocking at the door to buy them.

For many years Scottish-born players seemed to have had a big influence in English football. In the past, many of the bigger clubs, the League champions, FA Cup winners, seemed to have at least one Scot in their line-up. But that's not the case any more.

Celtic and Rangers have, without question, always been able to attract the majority of the cream of young players from north of the border, and possibly they still do. But of late, a few other clubs, such as Dundee United, Aberdeen, Hearts and Hibernian, have possibly had a better production line in terms of younger talent in the ranks, gaining a place in the first team.

Without a shadow of doubt, the old firm have always had the best choice of kids available to them. Well, I will admit, that most of my school friends wanted to play for either Celtic or Rangers; no other club was mentioned really.

The Bhoys and the 'Gers have been able to get more scouts covering different

Scotlands' U21 Coach Rainer Bonhof watches the players train at Douglas Park

towns and cities in Scotland (and the north of England) than anyone else. Literally thousands of young footballers have been monitored over the years. Hundreds of matches have been watched. The prospect of playing for the 'big two' was incentive enough for any boy or parent!

To me, playing for Celtic would have been a dream come true. It was something I always wanted to do, but it never materialised. I choose a club with a smaller set up with the hope of being able to get the chance of making progress into the first team sooner.

"The biggest worry is that the game of football goes in cycles. And at this present time, Scotland is not producing players. For whatever reason that is, I don't honestly know – but I don't think it's because the youngsters are staying in doors playing on their computers.

I think there is another angle on this. We are, and always have been, a small nation. We've qualified to play in several World Cups and that's a feat in itself.

The international teams of the past have been much maligned because they didn't go forward and continue to improve on the big stage.

Graeme Souness"

It was overwhelmed to be linked with Celtic as a youngster. But I chose a smaller club, as I thought I'd get a better chance . I was proved right in the end.

Celtic or Rangers were able to go out and buy top players as they wished, even youngsters at an early age. I thought this might hinder my chances of playing in the first team, so off I went to Dundee United in search of my glory.

There was a homely feel to the Tannadice set-up. Here was a top Scottish side, playing in the top Division who had just won the League championship with a relatively small squad and working to a tight budget, relying mainly on home produced talent, nurtured through the ranks. Therefore, my chances seemed far greater with Dundee United than they would have been at either Parkhead or Ibrox Park.

All the players would arrive at Tannadice every morning between 9.00 and 9.30a.m. to prepare and get ready to go to training at around 10.00am. The first team changed in the home dressing room and the young apprentices had to share the away team dressing room with the reserve players. This helped you to muck in with everyone and get an insight of what the top guys in the other dressing room might be like.

I raised the question with Kenny Dalglish, based on his expeience playing and managing in England, if he thought clubs like Dundee United would benefit from a academy?

"Why do you call it an academy?" he said.

"Below the age of 14, you don't need structure to the coaching but after 14 the boys need good coaching....

You have the school teachers and the organisation that would help them up to that age. You have to look at school kids today. Years ago there was thousands (of boys) that played the game.

Now you need to fill the gap and that requires good coaches.

The coaches need to pass their coaching certificates without costing them much money. At least that will give them some consistency in schools to coach the boys during the week."

Mixing with the players and training with them every other day helped me develop the physical aspect of the game far quicker than I had expected. It also gave me an insight as to what level I had to reach to make the grade as a professional footballer and how I had to conduct myself as a professional both on and off the park. Taking part in the odd training session with the first team helped me enormously.

As we were based inside the stadium and did not have any living accommodation close at hand, we all had to go our separate ways after training. Most of us had to walk a couple miles or so to our digs. I can assure you it felt even further in the winter. With relatively poor facilities at the time, the staff at the club couldn't really monitor our everyday condition as much as they would have liked. It was nothing compared with today with all the programmes that the S.F.A. have available.

Clubs like Dundee United didn't have a great deal of money to spend, especially on a decent youth set up. Our team comprised an assortment of schoolboy signings and triallists, and the majority of the games we participated in were listed as friendlies, mainly against other professional clubs, who themselves were trying to put together their own youth set up. We sometimes played against a lower based part-time league club like Forfar Athletic, usually on a Tuesday or Thursday evening when they should have been training. There weren't any

Things were a lot different in my playing days to what they are right now, totally different, in fact.

I started in the same era as Alex Ferguson and Billy McNeill. We played in the same inter-national schools team and youth sides together.

We all eventually found League clubs and as part of our 'breaking in' and 'learning process' we were farmed you out to a junior club.

Craig Brown

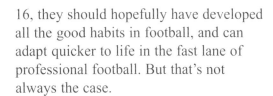

> *The danger now, of course, is at academies the younger lads feel as if they have arrived long before they've done anything, achieved anything.*
>
> *I just think there's a need for them to be grounded in more steadily, ensure their feet on firmly on the ground from the word go.*
>
> *Down here (in England) we spoil the kids with the facilities that are available at most academies. They are really fantastic. I wish they'd been around when I first started. In Scotland it's only Rangers, I believe, who have an academy that is top-notch. Academies have not worked yet – but they will.*
>
> *Graeme Souness*

professional academy leagues in those days like there are today.

I think there could be a finer balance in the way clubs work on their apprentices. They send them out to make the tea, get them to sweep up, clean the senior player's boots. Oh yes, they are put to work, but at the same time if they do what they're asked, then they will be treated well overall. I know that at times the young trainee can be, and is, treated quite harshly by the professionals but I have never heard anyone complain about it.

When you played in those scheduled youth matches, you would only know the names of say five or six of the lads you trained with on a daily basis. You were quickly told to find out the names of the rest of the players so that it would be a wee bit easier when calling for the ball out on the pitch. It was okay at times, but occasionally we found out that there were two Johns, two Joes, two Wills and so forth. And that proved rather difficult at times.

Some of these guys had been on trial at Dundee United and played in the same team as I did. Then, perhaps in the very next game, one or more would be on trial for the opposition, playing against us, having previously played with us. It was very confusing at times.

In my day, it was a huge honour for a young lad to be asked to go for a trial, but today it's a completely different ball game.

We were left to play and enjoy our football in our own way, but nowadays the advance on this means that many youngsters are being taught and coached the basics of the game at a very early age, some as young as six. When they reach the age of

Duncan Ferguson at Dundee United

16, they should hopefully have developed all the good habits in football, and can adapt quicker to life in the fast lane of professional football. But that's not always the case.

A committee, made up of five governors, organises the finances and after that, anything else that has to be paid out is the sole responsibility of each individual club, and some are struggling, believe you me.

The annual up-keep of a typical set-up isn't cheap. Blackburn Rovers are spending between £2m and £2.5m per season on their Academy to keep things ticking over at Ewood Park and have hundreds of kids associated with the club from age of seven upwards, costs an awful lot of money. In fact, there are lots of boys going to these type of set-ups in the hope of becoming the next soccer superstar, but only one or two will go all the way to the top… if they're lucky.

We all know, that money is not in the game anymore in Scotland.

So now, we really have to work hard at getting through this sticky patch and produce the talent that the fans deserve after so may let-downs.

Rangers was the first club in Scotland to produce a state-of-the-art facilities at their stadium and now Heart of Midlothian, with the aid of a national lottery funding through sportscotland, has put £1m into creating the Hearts Football Academy at Heriot-Watt University. Both clubs have certainly taken a giant leap forward.

The set up at Heriot-Watt University has also boosted community access to these top facilities. Hearts have daily access to six UEFA standard pitches, an indoor playing arena and top of the range fitness and medical facilities. There are those who question the value of the Centre of Excellence.

Craig Brown told me,

"In my two years as manager of Preston North End (2002-04), I used to see the younger players working away on the training ground and then watched the

Kevin Gallacher was the Scottish Brewers Sportswriters Player of the Month August 1986

SCOTTISH BREWERS

FOOTBALLER
OF THE MONTH
AWARDED TO

Kevin Gallacher

DUNDEE UNITED

Selecting Panel

Alex Cameron   DAILY RECORD
Gerry McNee   DAILY EXPRESS
Jim Reynolds   GLASGOW HERALD
Mike Aitken   THE SCOTSMAN
Ken Gallacher   THE SUN   AUGUST 1986

Under-18s queuing up for lunch after the professionals had been served.

I said to wee Billy Davies (my assistant at the time and later manager himself) not one of these youngsters will ever play for Preston. They don't look good enough.

He said: "What about Andy Lonergan – he looks to be a good goalie?

I replied: "I meant outfield players."

Today, it costs a club around £350,000 a-year to run a School of Excellence.

I said to him (Billy) politely, if we run a centre to cater for youngsters up to the age of 15 or 16, that doesn't bother me. It's when we have to coach and look after those aged 17 and 18 which bothers. If they are good enough, they should be full-time professionals, not running around in an academy-type complex.

Craig Brown (left) and Billy Davies at Preston North End

Just think, you (a coach) could have a lad who simply can't kick a hole in a paper bag; you are insuring him, scanning him, feeding him and probably arranging for his accommodation. Wouldn't it be better if we did away with all the preliminaries, started as before with an apprentice scheme and take it from there."

All the Scottish Premier League sides have youth teams and get one or two lads into the first team whenever possible, but now with Rangers and Hearts having created excellent academies, will other clubs, who are not perhaps quite financially-secure, be able to follow suit?

There are two sides to a coin. If a club can bring at least two players through every couple of years and then sell them on for a pretty substantial fee (say around £2m), then the answer is yes, the academy system is working.

But on the other hand, if a lower division club which is not really capable of producing that sort of talent at the moment, and can't justifiably place one of its youngsters into the first team, then the answer is no, it's not working all down the line.

Walter Smith told me;

"I think football academies could be the way forward in Scotland as they would benefit everybody. But it's like everything else, the number of youngsters who are entering the various academies at the minute are effected by what has gone on previously and will only have limited success if there are only a few enthusiasts. And that's what's happening.

It is horrendous. Okay, certain teenagers will, I know, aim to start out with say Arsenal or Manchester United, Liverpool or Blackburn, Celtic or Rangers. Most of them do so at the age is 15 and then, when they reach 17, they should, in theory, be ready for a career in professional football.

Unfortunately, that's not happening. I know there is a big drop in numbers attending academies and as a result, there's also a high percentage of players that don't make it as a professional.

There were about five or six of us who came up through the ranks and played in the first team (at Everton).

I think that you had a better level Kevin. I think your build-up was a slightly different to mine. I think the level of the player that develops now is not as high as it was say ten or fifteen years ago.

So what we are getting at the end of a course right now is a relatively high rate of those who don't make headway.

I don't know the exact figures, but I would estimate it's around the 75 per cent ...and that's after three years in an academy.

You are always going to get the exceptionally talented players coming through in England but there are a lot fewer than there used to be.

A Rooney, a Gerrard or a Cole, come through only very occasionally these days. I just think the overall skill factor is not there any more in youngsters."

However, being able to sell a young footballer for £2m or £3m, is not really commonplace these days in Scottish football. Although there are certainly quite a lot of teenagers registered with clubs in all Divisions, very few are regular first-team performers, many indeed, are just squad members, unlikely to be sold on for big money.

As football has progressed through the years, managers and coaches have been searching all over the world to see how different countries and clubs bring up their youngsters.

Holland is one country that has done

Former Scotland manager Berti Vogts during a training session

exceedingly well and as a result a lot of scrutiny is being placed on Dutch football right now. Most visitors are seriously interested in the success rate which has been achieved with regards to the number of younger players coming through the ranks.

Other teams in other countries have tried to emulate that, but have not quite reached the Dutch standard yet.

Holland has a specific set-up whereby players (two or more) become linked with one club from a very early age. They are all coached together and play in the same team, get to know each other's game thoroughly. The players grow up together, live, eat, socialise together, they become part of a football family.

Both Ajax Amsterdam and the Dutch national side have gone through a transitional period, as have many Scottish clubs and several more in England, a few big names like Arsenal, Chelsea, Manchester City, along with Reading, Hull City and others from the lower Divisions. All have introduced academies, encouraging youngsters to come along and hopefully make it possible for the clubs concerned to raise home grown players.

Today, throughout the world, not just Scotland, football is totally different. It's big the world over and there are, believe me, thousands of young boys (and girls, can't leave them out) enjoying the game. Teachers at school have their own subjects to manage… most of them as we all well know, aren't that interested in football. They don't want to stay behind after school hours. They know that all boys who want to play, will play - they'll find somewhere, some place to kick a ball around with their mates. Let in run. Boys will be boys and some, I guarantee, will become footballers.

I agree that we (Scotland) are not producing the sort of players we would like. But they will come through eventually. Barry Ferguson came out of the blue, so too did James McFadden and a few others.

Graeme Souness

Without doubt, Manchester United has probably had the most success with regards to producing its own players. As we know an sizeable batch of youngsters have come off the Old Trafford production line over the last decade or so, among them Ryan Giggs, David Beckham, brothers Gary and Phil Neville, Paul Scholes, Keiran Richardson, Wes Brown and Nicky Butt, to name just eight. And all came through the ranks more or less at the same time, progressing into the first team and winning trophies galore.

Sir Alex Ferguson just seems to have the knack of getting youngsters through to the highest level, having previously done it all at Aberdeen when he assembled a terrific team that went on to win the Scottish Cup, League championship and European Cup-winner's Cup in the space of only a few years in the mid-1980s.

And in truth, it was only a matter of time before he unleashed an array of exciting talent at Old Trafford. That was then, but in recent years, he admits that he has seen only a small number come through the ranks, certainly not at the pace he would have hoped for.

One major difference between apprenticeships and the academy nowadays, is this. The apprentices of yesteryear worked on their football the hard way. They cleaned player's boots, washed the dirty kit and learned all the necessary disciplines. They never got any extra help with regards to further education. Very rarely did a young player have something to fall back on, just in case he failed to make the grade as a footballer – and believe me, at least 17 out of 20 didn't (it could have been more) failed to make it as a professional.

The kids who are linked with football club academies right now, are released for one day's training to attend college and study for life after football. They don't serve a soccer apprenticeship in the same way as their predecessors did some 20 or 30 years ago. With a lot of the kids today, the respect and discipline has gone out of the game - sorry to say that, but it's true. Most of them start thinking they have made it as soon as they set foot inside an academy. Many of them fall by the wayside and end up working on the factory floor, in a shop, a superstore, market, even in a petrol station. The education side is there to help them, so if they don't progress into the big League, they have at least part of a career they can take up from their studies. Some do anyway.

The pressure on the manager of most football clubs today means they do not get the chance to see the progress of their young talent develop. As soon as the club starts to struggle in the League and all is against them, instead of promoting the couple of youngsters by placing them into the firing line for five or six games,

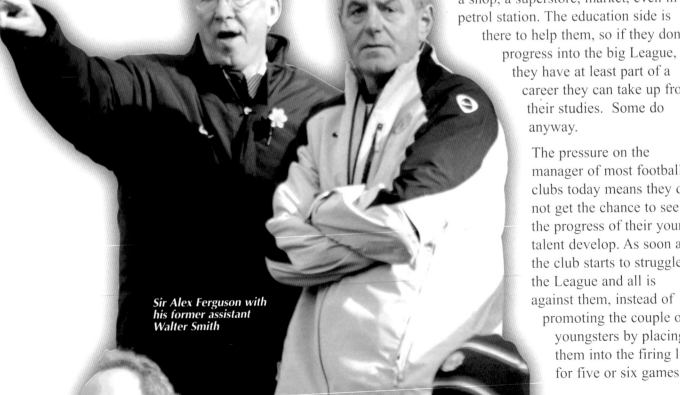

Sir Alex Ferguson with his former assistant Walter Smith

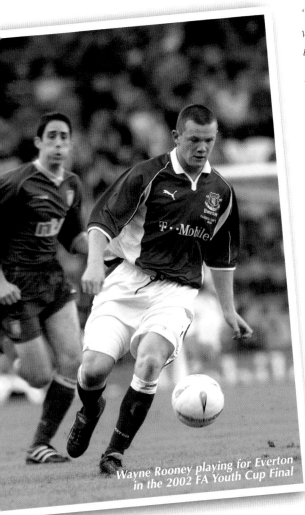

Wayne Rooney playing for Everton in the 2002 FA Youth Cup Final

"I think top clubs took all the cream they wanted before the soccer academy was introduced.

Around 18 boys, aged between 13 and 15, could all be signed up on schoolboy forms by any one club in Scotland and then, if two or more were deemed good enough, they were taken on as an apprenticeship come 16, leaving the remainder to look for a lesser named club, hoping to prosper by taking another route.

What's happening now, compared with the old 's' form and apprenticeship schemes, is that the system of today enables a club with an academy to take on some twelve to fourteen youngsters every year and hope that some make the grade.

You don't need to make a judgement and wait for a boy to reach the age of 16. He can simply slip through the net – leave whenever he wishes -and sign up for a bigger club.

Realistically three or four youngsters might just go on to make it - which is good for the game (and the academy concerned) but not for those others who would be left high and dry. This often happens when a smaller club doesn't get the ten to fifteen youngsters it had hoped for and all that are taken on are released.

It's back to square one, those that don't make it at the academy move to a smaller club or drift out of the game. It's happening in Scotland as well as in England, season after season."

the club goes out and buys or secures on loan ready-made players.

The best example occurred in England when Walter Smith was still manager at Everton. He had a young 16 year-old junior named Wayne Rooney knocking at the door to get into the first team, but because of the predicament that the club was in at the time, he couldn't afford to take a risk on him, Walter then left Everton with David Moyes taking over. He immediately took a gamble and gave Wayne his chance. From that moment onwards, Wayne (and indeed Moyes) have never looked back. Wayne of course was eventually sold to Manchester United for £27m. The money received by Everton paid off some of the club's massive debts, helped buy a couple of new players and help keep their academy going for at least another year.

As Moyes said;

Football club managers have the hardest job of all (in the game that is). They have to watch youngsters make progress, judge their potential, check to see if they are going to be good enough to make the first team better, and then, when the pressure is on, make a vital decision.

Jimmy Lumsden, a former coach at Celtic, told a story concerning Billy McNeill and his desire to win every single match as a manager no matter what level it was played at.

Charlie Nicholas

Tartan Turmoil
the fall and rise of Scottish Football

Recalled Jimmy:

"After Celtic reserves had defeated Clydebank reserves 4-0 with a team made up of several first team regulars, including David Moyes, Charlie Nicholas, Danny Crainie and Willie McStay, big Billy asked me the question, why did I choose to play so many senior players instead of using some of the younger kids like Paul McStay or Jim McInally? I told him that I felt we needed a stronger team on the day. 'Fair enough' replied Billy. So for the next match I fielded some of those young boys and we drew 1-1 with Morton reserves. I went into training the following morning and Big Billy said 'Hey Jimmy, why weren't the older lads playing yesterday?' I was caught in a catch 22 position, simply because Billy wanted to win every single match".

And as Moyes added;

"There are major differences between an academy and the various boys' clubs, such as were run by Aberdeen in the past. We need to improve the facilities in Scotland to enable us to produce better players for the future. There are pieces of Glasgow green that could be improved ten-fold. I am sure we could get 50 pitches on them. That would be great for the kids. There are other places too that could be utilised to play football on.

When I was being brought up, the pitches we used were on red ash.

I bet if you asked all the players from my era if they played on the red ash, they'd all say yes.

Maybe that's one of the reasons why defenders learned to tackle, because they wanted to stay on their feet rather than sliding or falling onto the ground.

It was nice to get a graze, a burn, a scrape on that red stuff.

Players also became better dribblers and passers of the ball, simply because the surface was flat and even. Sometimes when we played on a grass pitch, there were bumps and loose divots all over the place.

There were plusses and negatives, and in the main, I think it would have been difficult in Glasgow to find a decent grass pitch.

If we did, it was unbelievably lucky. The only time your team got to play on grass would be a Cup Final or were fortunate enough to represent your county at a junior or schoolboy level, you would play on a the ground of a major League club.

I can go back some 10 years or so to when the Scotland coach was Andy Roxburgh. He introduced 7-a-side football before anybody else.

We used to change overnight from having a big goal to shoot at to relatively wee ones in front of us. This was good. We had to work harder to create openings and this sort of training certainly benefited us youngsters no-end."

Jimmy Lumsden

To get the best out of the system, everything has to start at the top. Could the League limit the size of first and second team squad's as well as shifting the transfer embargo, just to let our

David Moyes

younger players get the chance and the experience playing in the big games?

John Collins told me about the set up they had at the French club, AS Monaco, when he was over there. There was a ruling in France that clubs were only allowed a

squad of twenty players and when they wanted to sign a new player they had to sell one first. Monaco had a couple of stars out injured plus one or two suspensions, so they had to bring in a couple of fresh faces from the youth team. Up stepped two young forwards named Thierry Henry and David Trezeguet. If the rules in France had been somewhat different then, who knows, Jean Tigana might well have gone out and bought a couple of players to add to his squad…and Messrs Henry and Trezeguet might never have got a chance.

But these two young French stars grasped the opportunity with both hands (and feet), showed what they could do, never looked back some eighteen months later became French internationals, going on to help their country win the World Cup in 1998 while Henry also became Arsenal's record scorer of all-time. So maybe if they bring in a different ruling at the top level, then who knows, we might start to benefit at youth level.

Two questions that need an answer are:

1. Has the growth of the Academies in England produced any more players than the original set ups?

2. Will we get more players through the system for the investment?

In my view the answers are clear:

1. They only need to find one or two, sell them on, make a profit and put some of the money received back into the academy for the next batch of youngsters to come through. It's as simple as that.

2. Having spoken to some managers they don't seem to think so. Is it just a benefit for the bigger clubs to throw out a wider net. Bigger clubs have always been able to attract good young players, so nothing has changed. Most consensus of opinion is that the academies are an expensive commodity.

*John Collins challenges David Beckham
in the Euro 2000 Play off 2nd leg*

chapter seven

TRAINING METHODS AND DIET

Everyone thinks that the professional footballer has a nice, easy life. They are wrong.

You are asked to turn up at the ground at a pre-fixed time on a Saturday lunch-time for a home game or report early in the morning if the team is playing away. You take part in the game, at least one-and-a-half hours of action, and then, after a shower or a bath, you travel back home, change your dress code and go out for a night on the town, with a beautiful girl hanging on his arm. It's different if you are a married man, by the way! You have a few drinks, possibly something to eat and then get a taxi home. And you pick up a healthy salary as well.

That may be the view on the terraces – but I can assure you, for some of us it was definitely not like that.

I think people forget, that during the week, a professional footballer works hard physically and mentally. He then has to play in at least one game (it's two early in the season and towards the end). At some stage you need to let your hair down and relax, putting football out of your mind.

Most of the time, that can only happen at the weekend, after the Saturday match, which, in truth, is no different to most people…a school teacher, a bank manager, shop worker, office clerk.

As a young boy, growing up in Clydebank, I worked really hard, playing football as often as I could, trying to get noticed.

I simply wanted to fulfil a childhood dream and become a professional footballer - and having watched lots of top stars in action, some live, some on TV, I often wondered why they didn't drink, smoke or get seen going out with girls.

I think I was a little too naive in those days and it was only when I signed for Dundee United that my opinion about professional (and amateur) footballers changed.

Yes, a lot of them might have done all of the things I have mentioned above. In the good old days it was more acceptable and they still worked unbelievably hard on the training pitches, mainly in the morning of each weekday, but occasionally after lunch as well.

A professional footballer's work starts on the training pitch. Although they do not always give the right impression, they do work exceptionally hard to achieve the level of fitness required to play at the top level. No pain, no gain, as they say.

Very few people are allowed to watch professional footballers train - it's different at some clubs, especially abroad. So spectators and supporters are not really able to get an insight as to what actually happens on a daily basis.

FACTFILE
DAVID MOYES
(born April 25, 1963 in Glasgow)

David took Preston North End F.C. to within a game of returning to the highest level of English league football for the first time in forty years but unfortunally lost in the play-off final to Bolton Wanderers F.C. He left in March 2002 to join Everton F.C., who were looking to retain their FA Premier League status. David turned their season around with nine games left. In the following season Everton's improvement continued as they moved towards the top of the table with a young Wayne Rooney making his debut.

David quickly established a great rapport with the fans at Goodison Park, referring to Everton as "The People's Club" soon after arriving. This phrase has been adopted as a semi official title for the club.

However, Rooney would leave Everton for Manchester United F.C. after a poor 2003/04 season, leading many pundits and experts to tip them as a favorite for relegation.

Due in no small part to Moyes coaching

The combination of a good diet with added exercise routines, requires great discipline at the professional level, something which is not often recognised by the general public.

Different managers at different clubs have their own regimes and theories, with some gaining invaluable knowledge by utilising specialist professionals. This option is often only available at the bigger clubs. The smaller clubs, with minimal budgets have to be far more scrupulous, which often restricts what they can actually achieve with their players

Playing football is not just about the creative side of the game. The difference between success and failure is often in the preparation.

When I left school and started training with Dundee United, back in the mid 1980s, the club was very meticulous in the way its players went about their coaching and fitness.

Manager Jim McLean had Walter Smith and Gordon Wallace alongside him on the coaching side, but the gaffer also had Ian Campbell as a part-time coach and Stuart Hogg as the club's running coach, just to help the lads with their fitness and stamina.

and managerial skills, Everton shocked virtually all of the so-called experts in 2004/05 by staying near the top of the table for most of the season.

They eventually finished 4th, assuring them a Champions League place.

A totally committed centre half, who led by example, played for Celtic, Preston North End and Shrewsbury Town.

Moyes' managerial style has been praised by several pundits, and great things are expected for him and Everton in future years if he can build upon the success achieved in the 2004-05 season.

Everton, however, made a poor start to the 2005-06 season. They went out of all European competitions by the end of September 2005 and after seven league games were last in the table, with only one win and only one goal from those games. Everton's season recovered and they were the first team to take points off Champions Chelsea in that season.

He was named the Premiership Manager of the Month for January 2006 during a long unbeaten run in the league. However the possibility of a place in the UEFA Cup faded after an indifferent spell and Everton finished mid-table.

David Moyes celebrates after winning the English Division 2 title with Preston North End in 2000

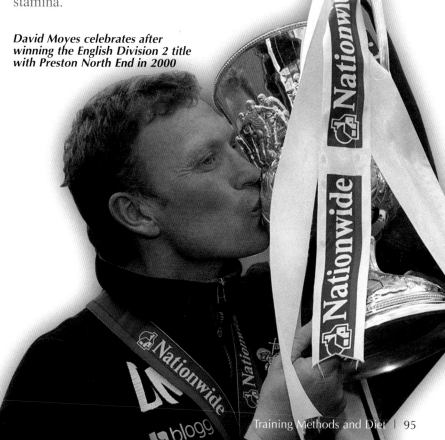

Tannadice Park - home of Dundee United

Going back to the time when I completed my first pre-season with Dundee United, I remember one of Jim McLean's favourite exercises was to take the majority of the registered players out for a day's training on the sand dunes at Monifieth. On one of my first outings to those dunes, I witnessed a few top players vomiting half way up the hill.

Thankfully, the boss was slightly kinder to the younger lads and we did not have to complete quite so many runs as the senior players!

> *It took me quite a while to bed in at Dens Park, but they were happy times. Gradually gaining experience, I rose up through the ranks and eventually became a member of the senior squad.*
>
> *Once you were an established professional you reported for training every morning, apart from Monday, no matter what. And that was it at as far as Dundee was concerned…and we still reached the semi-finals of the European Cup in 1963.*
>
> *Craig Brown*

Jim told me, that when he went to Dundee United they only had two youngsters signed up on 's' forms, one of them was Graeme Payne, the other Stevie Mellen.

Within no time at all, after several Sunday mornings watching boys' football, he decided to enhance the youth policy at the club and look create 'home grown' players.

He was well ahead of his time, but within a matter of months, the Lord Provost of Dundee granted us permission to open a new training facility and all of a sudden things were on the move.

I often think back to my time at Tannadice Park and remember all those strict training methods introduced by the coaches. It makes me think they were a little ahead of their time in relation to the methods they used.

To have the foresight to use a sprint coach such as Stuart Hogg, was a progressive move. I remember we had to run in and out of ladders to achieve "fast feet" and were trained using professional running methods. With all this hard, and dare I say it, strenuous work, I have to admit we seemed to make excellent progress.

Coaching exercises have not changed over the years….They have just progressed.

At the time, it seemed like something you would find in an army training camp. It highlights the initiative used by managers who were working and running a club on a shoestring budget.

Pre-season training will vary from club to club as managers and coaches come up with different ideas.

The management team at Dundee United regularly came up with something new and innovative. Sometimes you never touched a ball for the first two weeks of pre-season training. We simply concentrated on running…..round and round running tracks and across golf courses, and there were also treks along the beach and up and over those sand dunes!

Ten years later at Newcastle United, the pre-season training programme was based on running with the ball at your feet. I must admit, this made training (and indeed running) a bit more pleasurable!

Then, after two weeks or so, we would start playing friendly matches against selected opponents in preparation for the season ahead. Once the season got underway, however, the training programmes changed from those used in the pre-season schedule to gaining match fitness, and this was only achieved by taking part in a full-scale match. The general running was cut down, albeit only slightly, and the training became more technical with set-pieces, movement off the ball, formation play and general contribution from the players, emphasised in detail by the manager and his assistants.

Here is a typical example of a weekly session during my time with Dundee United.

• **Monday:** In the morning, you would go through a general warm up routine, which consisted of running round the perimeter of the pitch and doing stretching exercises for about 15 minutes. This would be followed by manoeuvring little five-yard passes, building up to 30 yarders, crossing and finishing inside and outside the box. And at the end, depending on how much time was left, you would compete in a series of small sided games, comprising five, six and sometimes seven players. In the afternoon, there would be individual coaching available for players in specialised positions, i.e. defenders on defensive positioning, midfielders on various passing drills, and forwards on movement and finishing. The goalkeepers were always kept active by the way.

• **Tuesday:** Morning warm up exercises as normal, with jogging and stretching, building up to sprinting. This was followed by a hard running session which could be anything from twelve by 100 yard sprints to four or six laps of the pitch, depending how the gaffer thought you were performing on the day. Usually the afternoon was left free.

• **Wednesday:** Normally the players would take the day off to rest (not shop with the missus), as most managers would say – although, having said that, if we had a game in the evening, then some players would go in for an hour or so, just to relax and flex their muscles.

• **Thursday:** The morning session comprised gentle jogging with stretching and warm up exercises, followed by passing, crossing and finishing, then more small-sided games, but this time you had to be much sharper. In the afternoon, certain players occasionally received individual coaching lessons, mainly of a light standard, but for the forwards (the strikers) we were always asked to practice our finishing, shoot on sight, shoot from any angle, shoot from distance, and we also had to head the ball…it wasn't all foot movement

• **Friday:** It was general jogging and warm-up exercises for the first part of the morning schedule, followed by some fun-inspired, short sharp, five-a-side games, before we went directly into sprint training, which was followed by a programme of set pieces - so that we knew what we were doing on the Saturday during the match – and after that it was a slow walk off the training pitch, into the dressing room, a shower and off home to relax before the big day.

• **Saturday:** Match day – report at the ground as and when required.

• **Sunday:** A day off.

> *You have to look at school kids today. Before, there were thousands that played the game. But you need to fill the gap and that requires good coaches.*
>
> *Kenny Dalglish*

Dundee United's training facilities at NCR Sportsground

I played in Italy for almost nine years. I don't know the way they train today, but when I was over there the training was certainly harder to what it was Scotland.

In Italy, players worked in groups - defenders with defenders, midfielders with midfielders, forwards with forwards. We did the usual running exercises, weightlifting (using proper weights), step-ups, jogging, arm and leg movements, stretching and so on. It was quite simple really, but strenuous at times.

This was a basic week in the life of a footballer (with Dundee United)… without any mid-week matches.

When you get youngsters telling you: "I canny kick it with my left foot so I ain't going to practice with my left foot". That gets you going, and annoyed Jim McLean said. "You have to use both feet in the game today, otherwise coaches will work on your weakness and you'll get crucified in a game.

Working harder on a weakness in your game is a priority."

On my travels from club to club, I have worked under several different managers, men like Jim McLean (at Dundee United), John Sillett, former England internationals Terry Butcher and Don Howe, along with Bobby Gould (at Coventry City), my boyhood hero, Kenny Dalglish, Ray Harford, Roy Hodgson and Brian Kidd (at Blackburn Rovers), Sir Bobby Robson (Newcastle United), Welshman Terry Yorath (Sheffield Wednesday) and Mick Wadsworth (Huddersfield Town), not to mention those on the international scene such as Andy Roxburgh and Craig Brown. And as I mentioned earlier, they all had their own different methods and routines.

I was so fortunate to have had the opportunity to take a little something from everyone mentioned above, as each had such an individual style of coaching and managing. If I look back to playing under Roy Hodgson at Blackburn

Rovers, even though his coaching sessions were very different to those of say Jim McLean, the theory is still the same.

Even though they were a decade apart, this again highlights the forward thinking of the coaching methods at Dundee United. Jim McLean may have ruled with an iron fist, but he always expected training to be done in a proper and professional manner, giving you as much information as he could in the hope you picked up a little bit along the way and carry the knowledge onto the pitch.

In comparison, Roy Hodgson's European approach was based mainly on concentration for the duration of the session. We had to wrap up well, as the sessions weren't the usual hustle and bustle of British training, but more a technical "stop start" approach. Here is an example of a typical week under Roy at Ewood Park.

Bobby Gould

Lorenzo Amoruso

• **Monday:** Usually the players took the morning off, but it was back for coaching session in the afternoon.

• **Tuesday:** Eleven players versus eleven; coaching, instructing and preparing the first team on how we were going to play; some functional work on crossing and finishing before taking the afternoon off, occasionally you came back for some individual coaching.

- **Wednesday:** Most players had the morning off; in the afternoon we would work out again, using 22 players (11 v. 11). The boss arranged a full 90-minute game, and the style and formation of our play was based on how the manager had assessed the opposition and how he thought they would play against us.

- **Thursday:** Another full scale match on the full pitch (11 v 11); here the boss shaped up the team he hoped to field on the Saturday, against the reserves, insisting that set pieces be practised and achieved the way he wanted.

- **Friday:** Normally, we were involved in nice and easy shadow play to make sure everyone knew their positions, set pieces were again practised with a lot more emphasis being placed on taking and defending corner-kicks and taking and facing free-kicks. And the team's penalty-taker also had a session on his own…just to give the goalkeeper some extra practice.

- **Saturday:** Match day and a talk in the dressing with the whole team present, to reiterate the positions of all set plays.

- **Sunday:** A day off – that's unless you were injured, and if that was the case, then you had to go to the ground for treatment and sometimes players who didn't participate over the weekend, were usually there as well, but only for a short time just to do some general training and keep-fit exercises.

As you can see, a lot of the training sessions concentrate on how you will play against the opposition and how the opposition will play against you on a Saturday. It was all good fun and very interesting – most of the time!

When you are a professional footballer, you put great demands on your body, as could be said for any professional sportsperson, especially the higher up you move in your sport. These demands are increased for any footballer when they manage to progress to the international stage. In my early days, I can remember having nine weeks off training during the close season. This seemed to be the perfect perk to the job, however

In Scotland you seemed to train as a group, a unit, altogether.

I understand that when you are with a club and in the first team squad, you work as a team, but to me, every player, every position is different and therefore I feel that certain players should train and work together. Meaning that a striker would need a practice, in the main, his shooting, a defending his heading and marking and a midfielder his passing. This to me seemed the right way forwards when I was in Italy but things certainly changed when I was based in Britain. When I was at Rangers, Alex McLeish started to use a different kind of training technique and eventually he chose to have his strikers and midfielders working together rather than the whole team training as one. It was okay in the end – but I preferred to the training methods we had in Italy.

Lorenzo Amoruso

Ex-Blackburn Rovers manager, Roy Hodgson during training

> *I ate and drank what was in the house, whether it was broth or tea, toast or biscuits. When I moved up to the professional ranks we had to order a pre-match meal and that was really the only involvement we had in respect of looking after our diet. The training and playing in matches did the rest.*
>
> *I usually had scrambled egg on toast for my pre-match meal. It started to become a ritual, nobody hassled you. But now, everybody has become far more aware of what they should be eating for nutrition and fitness purposes. This has been something that has changed fairly dramatically. It starts off at breakfast time and goes all the way through the day. Most players benefit from it, some don't bother...and people in the know, say realistically, that it's what you drink, fruit juices, milk, rather than what you eat is the best way forward.*
>
> *Walter Smith*

Walter Smith gives orders to his staff on the Scotland bench

as I moved up the ladder career wise, this became less and less, and it ended up being on average three weeks.

This may sound "normal", but you have to remember that this time off represents a whole year's holiday for the average footballer. In that time, they have to try to catch up on all their weekends, holidays and family time. Between the ages of 16 and 22, summertime seemed to be so long and sometimes the nine weeks off felt like a lifetime, but these were all our holidays in one swoop. Most of the time I played golf, but with some young players it meant even getting summer jobs for extra cash (haven't times changed!). When I began to represent Scotland all that changed.

After the European championships in Sweden '92 and England '96 I had approximately 3 weeks off to recuperate after the competitions. This would have been less had we progressed further. After the World Cup in France in '98, I managed to get eight days holiday in the south of France before I had to come back to England, I then had to have an operation on a double hernia.

If we analyse the fitness or injury status of many players after a long trophy winning season or on return from a major championship, you can see that a number spend the early, or in some cases most of the season on the treatment table. This is due to the fact that their body does not have enough time to rest to enable it to recover from such an intense period. This is often mentally very difficult for the player to recover from, as rather than building on previous success, you are subjected to a lonely and frustrating time in rehabilitation. With the progression of international football, they have gone from playing an average of maybe six games per season to almost double that. Having an international career can place an enormous strain, both mentally and physically, on the player as they combine playing for both club and country. Some professionals, are not able to find enough time for anything else and sacrifices must be made. Football is such a short career and most players are focused on trying to reach the pinnacle of the sport.

We trained and played hard, therefore burning off a tremendous amount of calories. To put the energy back into your system you would often eat anything that was edible from a chocolate muffin to a packet of crisps, not realising this was not actually the best method to recover your energy levels. In the past, the players would often eat and drink what they wanted, as diet was not at the forefront of everyone's minds, as it is now. Compared to other countries like Italy, whose diet of pasta, salad, lean meat, vegetables and olive oil has always been standard, we in Britain, and Scotland in particular, have had to work harder to move away from the traditional diet of fish and chips and curries. This may be an over simplification but none the less true. We have had to incorporate the continental way of eating. Football as a sport has become more athletic orientated in the last decade and as a result sports science has been introduced as a way of getting the best results from your body. Diet has had to change accordingly.

Football clubs with a larger budget have started to bring in sports science professionals to aid players and give nutritional advice. They would ask you to keep a diary of what you eat on a daily basis, to enable them to assess what your system is lacking and adjust it accordingly. The diary of many ex-players might read steak and chips, a pint (or two) of lager, a packet of crisps and a coke! Many players I played alongside in my early days struggled with fluctuating weight. Some even nipping off for a sauna before we took our morning weigh-in session! I, like many others, was lucky and easily maintained a healthy "playing weight". Food is the energy our body needs, and yes we do eat twice as much as the normal person but we need that amount to sustain enough energy to perform at such as high level. What we didn't realise in the past, was how significant diet was in enabling us to perform at our best. In saying that past generations of players, still managed to achieve top class performances. In today's game, the science aspect of diet and fitness has needed to improve to keep up with the way the game has changed.

Back in Dundee, when I lived in the digs, I would have breakfast, which consisted of a cereal and some toast. That would last me through to lunchtime by which time I would be starving. Lunch would be at the ground and consisted of pre-ordered sandwiches with a cup of tea or a cup of juice, then a mars bar just to fill in the gap. After we had done all our chores it would be back to the digs for tea with a decent sized portion of food depending on what the landlady had made. Then two hours later we would maybe go out for a take away Chinese. Fortunately for me this routine didn't last too long as I later moved out of digs and into family

The players canteen at Dundee United

Tartan Turmoil
the fall and rise of Scottish Football

Living near Stratford-upon-Avon at the time, we enjoyed dining out regularly and probably over indulged, but who doesn't when they are young?

At Coventry City's training ground there was a canteen and the chef, Roy, cooked the food and the two ladies there, Marie and Ros served you with your lunch. This was usually a choice of a baked potato with a topping, a pasta dish or a chicken dish of some sort.

At a bigger club like Blackburn Rovers, when I first arrived, we used to eat in the old stand in the John Lewis suite, because the stadium was being rebuilt. The players ate as quickly as possible just to get out and away from the ground. As Blackburn Rovers improved as a club, a new training facility was built and the canteen area was second to none. The choice for lunches put the local restaurants to shame. Different managers did different things. Although the food was reasonably healthy, it wasn't until the Roy Hodgson era that the healthy eating programme probably started. He brought in an Italian fitness coach Arnaldo Longeretti, who had ideas on how we should eat, drink and prepare ourselves.

accommodation with my Uncle Tom and Aunt Cathie and their kids. I shared a room with my older cousin Kevin! Yes there are two Kevin Gallachers! I couldn't complain about the way they fed me, but they could complain about me as I nearly ate them out of house and home.

As I got older and moved around clubs management had different theories on diet. You always got your weight checked on a weekly basis but some players were bigger than others and found it hard to keep their weight down. They thought they were eating and drinking properly, but we had no one there to educate us on nutritional things. We knew to an extent we had to eat carbohydrates and proteins and things like that, but nobody was there to explain how to put this into practice. To explain why we shouldn't have fry ups or drink too much beer. When I went to Coventry, I had not long got married and my wife Aileen looked after me with what we classed as healthy eating, which we would still combine with the odd take-away.

Sir Bobby Robson during a training session at Newcastle United

Sir Bobby Robson

Following Arnaldo's health and fitness regime, resulted in most of the players starting to lose body fat and for the first time ever, I was getting a six-pack. It took a while but we were still not getting to grips with his new health and fitness regimes.

At Newcastle United, lunches were similar to Blackburn with plenty of variety, including fish dishes. The fitness coach, Paul Winsper, made sure you had an energy drink as well. Sir Bobby Robson had a dining room rule. All the players had to be together and wait for Sir Bobby's say so before they could eat, at a specified time. Every day in the canteen, we were waiting for the teletext clock on the TV to give us the correct time so we could queue up to get our food. We would then sit down eat and have a chat. When we finished, we would wait for the manager to tell us what the next day's

agenda was. We were then finished for the day.

Preston was a smaller club and the variety of food was less with a much smaller choice. The food was good but not what I had been used to. Yes it was a decent selection but with a tighter food budget they had to make sure there was less food wastage.

At Sheffield Wednesday, because they were struggling financially, lunch was very similar to Preston. At Huddersfield, the purse strings were very tight and we were limited to a pasta dish, some bread and salad.

Match day preparations regarding food was always important, even in the early days, and varied from the every day diet. In the morning, I would have some toast and jam or a cereal or I would sometimes skip breakfast for a longer sleep and combine it with my pre-match meal. In my early days this would regularly consist of scrambled eggs, beans and toast. However, through the years my knowledge regarding nutrition increased and my body's needs changed so I introduced chicken and pasta to my pre-match meal.

The day before a match we found out was just as important as on the day, and we were encouraged to "load up" with carbohydrates, so usually pasta was always on the menu. Energy drinks have been introduced through many sports companies like Lucozade. Fitness coaches want you to drink these to help you re-balance the fluids in your body, drinking lots of water does help but the additives in the energy drinks just give you that little bit extra! When I was younger, I suffered a lot from cramp. At Dundee Utd, I would try salt tablets to help me get over cramp but this never seemed to work. It was only when a local Blackburn company, Sport in

Science, introduced me to a drink called electrolyte that I stopped having muscle cramps.

The game today is quicker and players are faster, because technology is changing all the time. Take the ball itself. I don't think any of the players today would like to play with the old style ball, with the laces to hold in the inner bladder. What a weight that must have been, especially when it got wet. Some of the older players have had neck and head problems later in their life and it was possible the ball had a part to play.

Football has to keep pace with change, and that change happens from the Boardroom to the training pitch. Whether we in Scotland have met the pace of that change outside the top two or three clubs, I am not so sure. From my experience though, unless we adopt the best training, and dietary practices, we can never attain the best levels. The harder you train and the better you look after yourself, the better you play. As Gary Player famously said.' the harder I practice the luckier I get'. This approach needs hard work and dedication from an early age.

Preston North warm up proir to the game against Dundee at Den's Park

Dutchman Micheal Mols of Rangers holding off Celtic's John Kennedy

chapter eight

FOREIGN IMPORTS AND MONEY

Ryan Giggs in action for Manchester United

Scottish clubs, for generations, have relied on home-grown and home produced players. It has been imperative for a lot of the teams outside the top flight to encourage youngsters to play football. The aim has been to nurture these players, and hopefully see them flourish and develop into senior pros.

The only problem has been, that as soon as these youngsters became strong enough and worthy of holding down a regular place in the first XI, one or two of the English clubs would come along, snap up the players (its never one at a time, always two, three or four) and whisk them down south. A significant batch of players from Scotland have packed their bags and headed south of the border, hoping of course, for a better and richer lifestyle.

I suppose in a way, the Scottish clubs are realistically deemed to be feeder clubs for their English counterparts. Thankfully, things have changed quite a lot in recent times. We don't have too many players nowadays going south and the players that do, mainly seem to be used as squad members or play in the lower Leagues, but what we are having is an influx of talent from abroad.

Some of them have certainly come for the money, while others arrived to just to prove people wrong (those who didn't think themselves good enough to make the grade in their country of birth). And of course, there have been the best of the rest. Players who believe they are good enough to perform in a completely different League set up, in a totally different environment.

When I first got involved in the senior side at Dundee United, we had a squad mainly made up of Scottish-born players with the odd dusting of English, Welsh and Irish. In fact, there were very few players from outside of the British Isles who were actually playing for any of the teams in the Scottish Leagues. At the time, the European rulings only allowed three foreign players into each team. However, some players, who were plying

their trade in England, and in various European competitions, were being classed as foreigners.

Take Manchester United's winger, Ryan Giggs, who represented Wales, despite playing his football in England, was classed as a 'foreign import' as UEFA and FIFA considered England, Scotland, Northern Ireland and Wales to be separate nations, not one solid body (Great Britain or the United Kingdom).

Because of this ruling, it meant that for a Scottish-born player, registered with a club down south (in England), would also be classed as a foreigner, unless he had either lived in the country (England) for a number of years or played in his club's youth team. This meant, in effect, that had been, or become, a 'nationalised' citizen. What a stupid ruling in my opinion!!!!

With the cost of certain British footballers steadily increasing over the years, this has led to some extravagant over-pricing in the transfer market. Transfer fees have gone through the proverbial roof. Amazing to think that Manchester United boss Sir Alex Ferguson splashed out £30 million for Rio Ferdinand in July 2002, making him the world's most expensive defender!!!!

> *Something that went through my head the first time I talked about signing a contract with Rangers was the money side of the deal. But in the end the money was probably the last thing I had in my mind when I actually signed the contract. At the time there seemed to be a big demand for Italian players with Serie 'A' clubs to come over and play in the U.K. I was looking forward to it as were several others. I could have earned perhaps a little extra more money by joining another established overseas club, but I was looking for a challenge and had no second thoughts about signing for Rangers.*
>
> *My idea was to try something new, enjoy a bit of Scottish culture. It was all worth it in the end - because I made so many friends there and I really loved it.*
>
> *Lorenzo Amoruso*

The so called big four in England, Manchester United, as well as Arsenal, Chelsea and Liverpool, and perhaps Celtic and Rangers can afford to pay out that sort of money to boost their squads. But there are many other clubs who simply can't afford the cash to recruit a certain player. This encourages many clubs to go out and buy a cheaper foreign footballer.

This is happening everywhere right now. Although Arsenal are not short of money, they went out and paid £4 million for the Brazilian World Cup winner Gilberto Silva. This was seen, at the time, as a very cheap signing, compared with the huge price paid by Ferguson for Ferdinand!!!!

Giberto Silva of Arsenal

Without doubt, the high prices which are now being asked for home-grown players is one reason why there is a massive influx of foreign players coming into the British market.

One other reason is the introduction of foreign coaches. Over the past decade, there have been quite a few who have entered the British game, several of them ending up with Scottish clubs. Ebbe Skovdal was recruited by Aberdeen, Vim Jansen and Dr Josef Venglos, in turn, by Celtic, the Italian Ivan Bonetti by Dundee, former Southampton defender Ivan Golac

by Dundee United, Harri Kampman by Motherwell and Dick Advocaat by Rangers.

Dr Josef Jenglos

Most of these 'foreigners', including Advocaat, who had done wonderfully well elsewhere, used their personal knowledge gained from links or associations with the clubs in their home country, to bring in quality footballers to the club they were managing. Advocaat signed at least ten overseas players for Rangers (to add to the half a dozen already at Ibrox Park when he took over from Walter Smith in 1998). His new recruits included Arthur Numan, Guivarchi, Giovani Bronkhorst and Andrei Kanchelskis and they blended in tremendously well, helping the Rangers complete the treble (the Premier League title, the Scottish Cup and League Cup).

The following season he boosted his squad by signing Michael Mols from his home country, Holland, and won the League title and the Scottish Cup again while also reaching the group final of the Champions League.

The Dutchman certainly did an excellent job with Rangers and I am certain that many other Scottish clubs followed his lead by importing more foreign players than they would have liked, simply because the transfer market in the U.K. had gone through the roof. It seemed more practicable to pay a smaller fee (certainly

Andrei Kanchelskis

consequently struggled on the pitch. Other players have lost confidence and results have taken a turn for the worse. Nine times out of ten, the unsettled foreigners depart and it's back to square one for the manager.

I am aware that bringing in some of these foreign guys has made a lot of people learn a lot more about the different cultures of World and European football. They obviously bring with them, a completely different style of football, a bit of mystery and also a lot of glamour to the Scottish Premier League. They've also been influential in making the young Scottish player rethink his approach to football and possibly to life overall.

The way they approach the game is different; the way they eat and drink before matches is something new; the way they look after their own bodies, their diet, their fitness and their individual skill is also so very different to what the Scots are used to. Yes, there's no doubt, that bringing in better foreign imports, quality footballers, players who've proved they can perform at the highest possible level, has changed a lot of things in the

> *Foreign players have helped without a doubt.*
>
> *Any players with ability can and often is a positive influence on an up-and-coming young footballer.*
>
> *Take the likes of Eric Cantona, Thierry Henry, Henrik Larsson...all great footballers...and the younger fans looked up to them.*
>
> *Walter Smith*

Brian Laudrup

Dado Prso

Nacho Novo

Scottish game today.

Take Dundee United for instance. During the 1989-90 season, the season I left Tannadice Park to sign for Coventry City, there were four foreign players at the club - a Dutchman, Freddy van der Hoorn, a Finn, Mixu Paatelainen, Miodrag Krivokapic, the Yugoslav and Peter Hinds from Barbados. Three of them were held in high esteem (in their home country) which at that time was not a bad ratio. Dundee United had been introducing foreigners to Scottish League and Cup football prior to that and many more would arrive in the future.

The first overseas players to sign for my old club, Dundee United, was the durable Finn Dossing who was recruited from Danish football, and Orjan Persson, a Swede, who were both brought over by then manager Jerry Kerr.

They had made their senior debuts in their home countries back in 1964, so they were very experienced campaigners. Orjan was also the first Dundee United player, along with fellow countryman Lennart Wing, to win a full international cap. There was also another foreign player at the club named Mojens Berg, also a Dane, who had joined around the same time as the others....to start a foreign legion at the club.

Tartan Turmoil

Many people argue that Scotland has been handed the short straw over the years with regards to foreign players. With precious little money to go around, most clubs (certainly those from outside the Premier League) have secured the services of several players on a cheap labour policy. As a result, by getting them signed up for practically nothing in terms of a transfer fee, it clearly indicates (to me) that managers are saying that the country's younger players are not good enough to handle or indeed make progress in top flight football.

Is it just a case of there being too much pressure on the management for instant success, compared to our English counterparts who, with the added attraction of finance, can attract some of the world's best players? The money generated from TV, the lucrative sponsorship deals and advertising revenue (as mentioned previously) does, without a shadow of doubt, considerably help most of the top Premiership clubs. But we must remember, and consider, that not all the football clubs are that rich.

We are all, it seems, quite happy to talk about playing in the top Division (in Scotland, England or wherever). We mustn't forget the smaller clubs however who have to scrap hard and long to survive in the lower regions of domestic soccer. This is especially true in Scotland where a lot of the clubs are part-time

organisations and their players have another daily job to do, as well as playing football, so that they can earn a decent living.

I know that many footballers linked with the likes of East Stirling, Albion Rovers, Montrose, Elgin City and Arbroath, train perhaps two or three nights a week, having grafted for eight hours during the day as drivers, factory workers, engineers, schoolteachers, office clerks and so forth. These men simply love playing football and thoroughly enjoy the sport. They are the salt of the earth as far as I am concerned…

Going back to our foreign brethren….Some of these players are worth their weight in gold in their own countries, but very few of them have come to Scotland and lit the heather alight. Over the course of time, nearly every club who has held membership in the Scottish Premier League, has, at some point, signed a foreign player (or two, or three). They have come from all over the world - from North and South Africa, from South America, from the Caribbean, certainly from Scandinavia and most of the main European countries, like France, Holland, Germany, Italy, Spain and Portugal, even Greece and Turkey.

Most have played their part, whether small or large, in their club's search for League or Cup success. Some have been

Miodrag Krivokapic

> *I don't know too many players who have really failed to settle in Britain or indeed, in other countries. I think it's to do with the fact that when you go to a different country, a different environment, you need to adapt, and you need to approach the game in a different light, try and learn a new language, especially the important words, and get to know the everyday habits of the British people, more so of those in Scotland. That was not easy, but I got by.*
>
> *Lorenzo Amoruso*

unable to make the grade, others have excelled. There have, I know, been some very average foreign players associated with several Scottish clubs as well as several expensive signings.

Dundee United equalled the club's transfer record when they signed Victor Ferrera from San Lorenzo for £350,000 in 1991. He spent just two years at Tannadice Park and managed to play in just 35 competitive games before jetting off to Japan.

There were many more players like Ferrera who actually came into a club and as a result disrupted (halted) the progress of a young up-and-coming Scottish player, preventing him from getting a game in the first team. Signing players from other nations is realistically a big, big gamble.

Take the first Brazilian to appear in the Scottish Premier League.

His name was Sergio Gomes, a centre-forward, who arrived at Tannadice Park under good recommendation in 1995. He managed to score three goals in 14 games and stayed for just six months, before returning home.

Another player, Walter Rojas, comes into the same category. An Argentine, he was recommended to Dundee United by an agent in London. Everything was carried out officially. He signed the appropriate papers but later it emerged that United had been a victim of duplicity. Rojas was well short of the required standard, and to say the least, his stay at Tannadice was short-lived!!!!

This is just one clear example of what can happen when recruiting a foreign footballer who is inexperienced and relatively an unknown quantity.

And believe me, there have been many more who have drifted across the Irish and Atlantic seas to try their luck in Scottish football and have failed miserably. In the weeks and sometimes months they were training and playing with the club they had signed for, you could have had another youngster in the same sort of position, mixing in with the senior professionals, gaining valuable experience and feeling confident of making it into the world of professional football.

The way the structure was set up initially, clubs were not allowed to bring in foreign players on trial. Therefore, the way round this would was to sign the player in question on a short-term deal with a get-out clause inserted in the contract.

The player, in effect, would be 'signed' for a trial period (possibly for just a one month trial) and that gave his manager plenty of time to see if he was good enough to be taken on as a full-time professional with a longer contract.

If, of course, the manager and his coaching staff didn't think much of their trialist during his time with the club, then the short-term contract would be torn up and the player involved was free to move on. The only downside to this sort of deal was that the manager had to announce to the club's supporters, and also the media, that he had signed a new player, a foreigner.

And I do know, from experience, that most of the time, the boss would get

Walter Rojas (left) and Viltor Ferrara

crucified by the fans for making a bad signing.

In November 1996, I recall Southampton manager (and former Rangers player-boss) Graeme Souness, signing a relatively unknown Senegalese player called Aly Dia on the recommendation of the Liberian international George Weah, who starred for AS Monaco, Paris St Germain and AC Milan.

He handed him his debut as a first-half substitute in the Premiership game against Leeds United. Embarrassed with what he saw, Souness whipped him off after just 14 minutes and Dia quickly disappeared from The Dell. "He was useless, a joke" said the annoyed Souness.

I think that taking a gamble on an unknown foreign player is totally wrong.

I would say it would be far better to take a gamble on one of the youth team players, the best teenager, one who cost the club nothing in terms of money.

If the gamble fails, okay, the club loses absolutely nothing. If it comes off, then it's a massive bonus to all concerned, no questions asked. And in the long run, that very same youngster may well become the team's star performer, the fans' idol, and have every big club knocking on the door for his signature.

Former Rangers boss Graham Souness agrees with me that foreign players are preventing Scottish youngsters coming through. He told me;

"With foreign players joining Scottish teams the development of some youngsters has been restricted but if they were already in the team before the foreign import arrived, you would continue to play them.

It's all down to the club and the manager. If he feels he's under pressure, then sometimes he introduces a new face to spark things up a bit.

He can still play some of the young players, groom them along slowly, allow them to gain experience by playing alongside an established and more experienced professional, like a foreigner.

I don't think a manager can, or will, make a decision on a young player straightaway.

He'll give him a decent chance. After perhaps four or five matches, if he hasn't shown too much of an improvement, then he can have second thoughts, possibly loan him out to a lower League club.

There's a lot of luck involved in football. Being in the right place at the right time is crucial.

Look at Dundee for instance. They got relegated at the end of the 1993-94 season, finishing bottom of the Premier League despite having quite a few foreigners in the squad, including Pageaud, Wieghorst and Vrto, who were retained.

Manager Jim Duffy was delighted when his side bounced back at the first attempt."

The conveyer belt at Tannadice Park was always running, and at that time lots of younger players were already coming through Jim McLean's splendidly-organised School of Excellence. The only problem the gaffer had was because of all the success the club had achieved, he was under a wee bit of pressure, not just to produce the young talent for the future and play them in the first team, but first and foremost, he had to select a team capable of going out and winning football matches.

There were lots of teenagers leaving school who desperately wanted to become footballers. They wanted a trial, the opportunity to show what they could do, even at a young age. The manager's in-box on his desk was always full of letters from youngsters asking for a trial!!! He delegated others to sort this out – but this was just what the club wanted – young boys, all wanting to become professional footballers.

A few made it, hundreds didn't. But if you check through the individual careers of most of the players, they all had to start at

> *Sometimes when you sign a foreigner, you think you are getting a ready-made footballer, which is not always the case.*
>
> *Craig Brown*

the bottom and climb the ladder slowly. Some of them shot up there like nobodies' business – great for the club – but others sadly left bitterly disappointed. Those who were signed by the club (the majority as apprentices) were obviously expected to make some sort of progress, show improvement, develop their skills and eventually be in a position to challenge for a place in the intermediate side, then the second XI and finally the senior side.

It was all about gaining experience, and that's where the mix of youth and experience, as well as maybe quality imports, came into good use.

Most clubs had at least a couple or three experienced campaigners, seasoned professionals who knew the game inside out. And there was of course the manager himself, plus his assistant and possibly a coach there to help as well.

There is always some sort of pressure on the manager. He has to decide what's best for the future of the club. Does he go out and buy a ready made player, does he recruit a foreigner, a Scotsman, or a Brit? I know that a lot have done that, signed a quality professional who's been in the game for quite some time, but also I know of other managers who have taken the different route and gambled on a young player.

It is not always bad news when you bring in a foreign player. I admit, there have been some quality footballers as well as some bad ones.

The good ones obviously stand out and are immediately noticed, quickly become household names and know they'll be talked about years after they've retired….such as those previously mentioned like Dossing, Prytz, Larsson, Moravcik, Laudrup, Caniggia and so forth. This type of players is a pleasure to watch. The skill just oozes from them and as a youngster you would be able to learn something from each and every one of those guys.

The problem is a simple one. We don't give the foreign players enough time to settle into their new environment, while at the same time they are not allowed, to a certain extent, to show off the talents for which they were initially brought to the club. They are supposed to give the fans the entertainment value they crave. Then, again, if you want them to hit the heights immediately on arrival, and they don't succeed, having not had enough time to settle, then that could be disastrous.

I know of a few players, some mentioned earlier in the book, who joined a club from a foreign source, failed to settle in his new surroundings, struggled on the pitch, felt homesick and returned home in double-quick time. It happens all the while, not only in Scotland but all over the world where football is played.

I was fortunate enough, late in my career, to have trained with the Palermo Under-21 side, an Italian outfit, based on the island of Sicily. This was a great opportunity to sample for myself what it is like to train with other lads that didn't speak the same language.

This was in the summer of 2002, just before I switched my allegiance to Huddersfield Town, the club with whom I eventually ended my career.

I went over to southern Italy and spent a week coaching and training with a young Palermo team. What went on over there certainly opened my eyes and helped me understand why it was so hard for a foreign player to adapt to the British game.

Henrik Larsson says goodbye to the fans after his last ever match for Celtic

a smart tracksuit, looking authoritative, he would call out the colour and expected us to react and sprint as hard as we possibly could towards that colour which was visible on a marker ahead of us.

I was behind these kids by about one yard by the time my brain kicked in and told me what the translation was for red, black, white and yellow. Then, once I understood, I dashed straight down the 30-metre course towards the marker. In the 2nd race the kids couldn't believe how fast I ran, especially for an old thirty-six year-old, as I left them behind - only because I didn't have to understand any Italian words other than go!

It just goes to show that language is the most important barrier you have to break down – especially when you want to pursue a footballing career abroad.

Settling into a new lifestyle (anywhere other than home) can be quite hard. Finding the correct area to live in, the right house, being away from the family, these are the biggest draw backs for a footballer, more so if you are married and have young kids.

Settling the children into a brand new school is a major upheaval. Many foreign players just come to the U.K. for the money, and once bedded in, learn that there is more to life than money. Many of the players love the Scottish culture and make new friends very quickly.

The way the Italians organise their coaching and training sessions is completely different to how their British counterparts prepare things.

They invariably start by placing you into a chosen position. Would-be strikers are coached together, do their heading, shooting, running all in a group. Defenders get coached on the lines of

There was of course, a language barrier that had to be overcome. And then there was the football side as well and trying to adapt to the country's environment. Football at the end of the day is a multi-nation sport and if you want to succeed then you will have to overcome many hurdles to enable you to reach your goal.

I didn't realise by not speaking a little bit of the language it took away one yard of my game. It was most noticeable when I was racing some of the kids at sprints. The Italian coach organised a session whereby we had four different colours - rosso, negro, blanc and giallo. Dressed in anything defensively-minded, tackling, heading, marking, kicking, positional sense and so forth. And the midfielders work together as a unit on attacking and defending, passing, shooting occasionally, and generally working with each other on various strengths and weaknesses, whether it was with the ball or in the form of running and positioning. It was a major part of their make up and was very similar to the way Roy Hodgson did his coaching at Blackburn.

I spent a couple of seasons under his regime at Ewood Park and learned a lot more about the game than I could imagine. For many years now I think the British game has been dominant physically and the foreign players have learned more about that aspect of the game, emphasised clearly in the way the former Celtic striker Henrik Larsson handled himself when he was at Parkhead. He certainly picked up more skill on the technical side of the game, improved his shooting ten-fold and became a world-class footballer in a relatively short period of time.

Guys like

Lorenzo Amoruso said:

"I was really surprised about the way they played the game in Scotland. Players never give up, even in games when we were leading four, five or six nil. They kept going to the end, it was really tough. When Rangers won the treble in 2002-03, our last League game was against Dunfermline Athletic at home.

We were level points with Celtic who were playing Kilmarnock, and I think we had a slightly better goal-difference. Therefore, everyone was ready to give their all, to play for 90 minutes and more and we were determined not to let anything go wrong.

It was an amazing match. Confidence was so high that everything we touched turned to gold. We won 6-1 to keep Celtic (who won their 4-0) away from us and of course clinched the title in style.

I recall that when were winning 3 –1, then 4-1 and 5 –1, Dunfermline wouldn't give up despite it being the last game of the season and realistically they had nothing to play for other than pride, although they were 5th in the table.

Normally when a team enters its last game of a long

Lorenzo Amoruso celebrates after winning the Scottish Cup in 2003

campaign with nothing really at stake, certain players will not, I am sure, give their all, but in Scotland it's different.

Players love their football, win draw and lose, and that's what I enjoyed about my time in the Scottish League.

In Italy if a team had virtually finished its match programme, were comfortably placed in mid-table with nothing to play for, certain players (no names mentioned) would simply go out onto the pitch, perform at a walking pace (or as near as), just waiting for the final whistle from the referee.

It was ridiculous. I didn't like it one bit. There are good and bad things about Italian football. The way players think, the way they approach the game, the way coaches work, the tactics, the match preparation, the small things, it all makes a huge difference in the end.

I know sometimes people will say that Italian football can be boring at times."

Bringing in players from a foreign country has probably helped to enhance Scottish football as a spectacle, but in no way has it helped the national team's cause. Perhaps the greater mobility of foreign football talent will make us rethink our attachments and views of the national side with some people actually questioning the validity of having a national team. After all, Chelsea could probably now beat England and either of the old firm teams could probably do the same to Scotland.

However, by increasing player mobility it might have strengthened national team attachments, but as far as the diehard

supporter is concerned, who follows his beloved country through thick and thin, all over the world, he has to wait around, until the national team manager/coach assembles his best players for an international match, before he can go out and watch his favourites in action.

In reverse, fans from other countries are now following their favourite stars, currently playing in the Scottish Premier League, and this has the effect of raising the profile of Scottish football abroad. What has happened in the Scottish game with foreign players is not exclusive to Scotland it is the same worldwide.

Supporters travel thousands of miles to watch their favourite player take part in a competitive match. There are regular flights from many of the Scandinavian countries into Glasgow for the weekend fixtures, and likewise from France and Italy. And the same can be said of similar excursions from European airports to Manchester, Liverpool, Birmingham and London.

Aeroplanes and ferries full of excited supporters wanting to keep in touch with their favourite players!

Fans and clubs in Scotland, as do their neighbours south of the border, want their cake and eat it. There is a conflict between club and country for sure. Clubs want to have the best players now. They want instant success. As for the big two, they have to aim to win the title and do well in Europe. Foreign players (including English imports in that) have been an essential ingredient for both clubs. The downside to this is that hardly any players in the latest Scotland Squad for Japan came from either Celtic or Rangers. This issue is not just a Scottish one. South of the border I am sure some of the best players in the English Premiership, such as Carlton Cole at Chelsea, would have played regularly, but there are so many foreigners in the game, they end up being squeezed down the pecking order.

It's the same in Scotland.

*Kenny Miller in action
against Belarus*

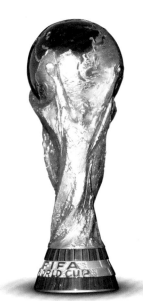

chapter nine
WORLD CUP YEARS

It is probably the best pub conversation ever – when the Scotland National team is under scrutiny… and the questions rain thick and fast.

How good was Jim Baxter? Was Dave MacKay a better midfield player than Graeme Souness? Is Kenny Miller the new Kenny Dalglish?

We all talk about football comparisons, we all have different opinions and we all want to state them. That's life… and the same sort of thing will go on for years.

People, especially the older ones, will always argue that players from yesteryear were a better breed than those of today, but what we are seeing is the changing face of world football.

Would the pace of today's game have helped Denis Law become a better player and still score as many goals? Would it have helped Jimmy 'Jinky' Johnstone cross the ball better?

That is why we all love the sport; there are so many questions to answer, so many points of interest, it's fascinating.

All youngsters – if they are interested in the game of course - have dreams as boys of becoming professional footballers and reaching the top rung of the ladder. Some achieve their goal and represent their country in the World Cup. Some fail and go away bitterly disappointed, thinking what might have been.

Scotland first tasted World Cup football in 1954 in Switzerland. Undefeated in three pre-tournament friendlies, they lost 1-0 to Austria in the opening encounter in Zurich and were then hammered 7-0 by Uruguay in Basle in match two. Tommy Docherty played in both of the games and fifty-odd years later he still recalls that humiliating defeat against the Uruguayans. He said: "We played horrible. We were lucky not to have conceded twelve goals."

Andy Beattie (Huddersfield Town) was in charge of the team in Switzerland and actually he quit shortly before that Uruguay debacle (following an internal dispute).

Four years later in Sweden, Scotland – the only country to participate without a manager, due to the tragic circumstances surrounding Matt Busby who was badly injured in the Munich air crash – were led by senior trainer Dawson Walker.

Despite an early injury to Stewart Imlach, Scotland held Yugoslavia to a 1-1 draw in the opening game in Vasteras, Jimmy Murray of Hearts having the pleasure of scoring his country's first-ever goal in a World Cup finals tournament.

A 3-2 defeat by Paraguay in Norrkoping in their second game when they fielded a lightweight team against brawny and tough opponents, meant that the Scots had to beat France in the third match to progress through to the next stage. They battled hard but went down 2-1. It might have been a different story had Charlton's John Hewie not missed a 67th minute penalty, but the French had goal scoring genius Juste Fontaine in their ranks and in the end his lethal strike decided the contest, despite Sammy Baird's late consolation effort.

It was to be another 16 years, before the blue and white colours of Scotland would be in evidence again on the world stage.

Missing out on qualification for the 1962, 1966 and 1970 tournaments was a bitter blow to some of the great players who were around at that time. Stars who would surely have made a major impact in those tournaments, such as goalkeepers Bobby Clark and Bobby Ferguson, the elegant and graceful Jim Baxter (what a player he was), full-backs Eric Caldow and Tommy Gemmell, hardened defenders John Greig, Sandy Jardine, Ron McKinnon and Billy McNeill, cultured wing-halves Billy Bremner and Paddy Crerand, Tottenham Hotspur's brilliant inside-right John 'The Ghost' White who was tragically killed by lightening on a golf course, wingers Bertie Auld, Willie Henderson, the fiery but lively Willie Johnston, bullet-shot Peter Lorimer and the tricky Davey Wilson, the skilful Ian St John, goalscorer-supreme Denis Law and proven strikers Colin Stein, Joe McBride, Steve Chalmers, Alan

"People have asked me if I think the Scottish game has changed a lot over the years.

Yes, it has changed without any shadow of a doubt. There's a lack of quality right now, and that's down to lack of practice.

Jim McLean"

Gilzean, who was also a terrific header of the ball, Bobby Lennox, silky Alex Young and Willie Wallace.

If they had all been around together what a team Scotland could have had!

Surprisingly, though, Scotland have never really set the world on fire in competitive football, despite having so much talent to choose from, certainly during the 1950s, '60s and early 'seventies. The Home International Championship was won a few times, but with regards to the World Cup (even the European Championship) nothing really was achieved, other than qualification.

Having said that, the team performed with a lot of guts and determination in Argentina in 1978 and were perhaps a shade unlucky not to qualify from their group, which contained the 1974 runner's-up Holland who, in fact, were defeated 3-2 by the Scots, Archie Gemmill scoring a wonderful individual goal.

It was the same old story four years later in Spain when once again the Scots thought they might just squeeze through from their group, especially after beating New Zealand in their opening fixture. But defeat at the hands of mighty Brazil and a draw against the USSR, meant they had to fly home from Spain earlier than anticipated.

And annoyingly, it was a touch of dejá vue once more in the Mexico World Cup finals of 1986. Two defeats, against Denmark and West Germany, and a draw with Uruguay was all the Scots could manage and they returned home with their tails between their legs.

It seems to me that over the last twenty years, since Spain 1986, Scotland has struggled to make any sort of impression in the qualifying stages of the World Cup competition.

Why that is, I simply don't know – and a lot of other folk feel the same.

Having qualified for the 1974 World Cup finals in Germany for the first time since 1958, Scotland were drawn in the same group as Brazil, Yugoslavia and Zaire.

Willie Ormond was the team manager and his squad comprised the following 22 players:

SQUAD LIST
WORLD CUP 1974 - GERMANY

1. David Harvey   GK
2. Sandy Jardine
3. Danny McGrain
4. Billy Bremner
5. Jim Holton
6. John Blackley
7. Jimmy Johnstone
8. Kenny Dalglish
9. Joe Jordan
10. Davie Hay
11. Peter Lorimar

12. Thomson Allen   GK
13. Jim Stewart   GK
14. Martin Buchan
15. Peter Cormack
16. Willie Donachie
17. Donald Ford
18. Tommy Hutchison
19. Denis Law
20. Willie Morgan
21. Gordon McQueen
22. Eric Schaedler

Scotland opened the campaign with a hard-earned 2-0 win over the relatively unknown African side, Zaire, in front of 30,000 fans in Dortmund. Joe Jordan and Peter Lorimer scored the goals in the space of six first-half minutes after David Hay had struck a post. After a floodlight failure, Lorimer hit an upright but the narrow victory was not what the Scots wanted...victory should have been by a much bigger margin than two goals, the newspapers blaming the skipper, Billy Bremner, for not encouraging his players to attack in numbers against one of the weakest country's in the tournament.

After some hard training sessions and a few dressing room pep-talks, Scotland then went out and held Brazil to a goalless draw before a crowd of 62,000 in Frankfurt, goalkeeper David Harvey producing three superb saves while Sandy Jardine was as solid as a rock in defence.

However, next up it was Yugoslavia who had thrashed Zaire 9-0 in their second game. Brazil were expected to beat the Africans comfortably (at least by three goals) in their final group game, and therefore Scotland knew they had to beat the Yugoslavs to stay in the competition.

The white-shirted Scots gave a good account of themselves in front of a 56,000 crowd in Frankfurt. Learning that Brazil had beaten Zaire 3-0, they went all out for victory but a late goal – after Jordan's opener – sent Scotland home after a 1-1 draw.

Four points from three games was not enough, yet Scotland surprisingly was the only unbeaten nation in those 1974 finals.

The Scotland party flew back home to a tremendous reception. There were about 10,000 fans at the airport to meet what was seen to be one of the best squad of players the country had ever taken to a World Cup finals.

But deep down, it was again very disappointing for all concerned, and in simple terms, Scotland weren't good enough on the day despite some plucky performances. End of story.

This was the final group two table at the 1974 World Cup.

Team	P	W	D	L	F	A	Pts
Yugoslavia	3	1	2	0	10	1	4
Brazil	3	1	2	0	3	0	4
Scotland	3	1	2	0	3	1	4
Zaire	3	0	0	3	0	14	0

Four years later it was off to Argentina for the 1978 World Cup, and this time it was Ally Macleod's Tartan Army who carried the hopes of Scotland.

Gathering together at Hampden Park for a big send off, the squad was buzzing, had high hopes of doing well and engineered by the effervescent MacLeod, they were quietly confident of doing something unexpected!

There were a few new faces on view as the party - wearing smart, navy blue tracksuits - walked around the Glasgow

*Dave MacKay and Billy
Bremner 'square up'*

Kenny Dalglish celebrates scoring for Liverpool

stadium,
acknowledging the applause from a wildly, enthusiastic crowd prior to jetting off to South America.

These were the 22 players MacLeod chose to take with him:

SQUAD LIST
WORLD CUP 1978 - ARGENTINA

1. Alan Rough   GK
2. Sandy Jardine
3. Willie Donachie
4. Martin Buchan
5. Gordon McQueen
6. Bruce Rioch
7. Don Masson
8. Kenny Dalglish
9. Joe Jordan
10. Asa Hartford
11. Willie Johnston

12. Jim Blyth   GK
13. Stuart Kennedy
14. Stuart Forsyth
15. Archie Gemmill
16. Lou Macari
17. Derek Johnstone
18. Graeme Souness
19. John Robertson
20. Bobby Clark   GK
21. Joe Harper
22. Kenny Burns

Unfortunately Scotland opened the 'Mundial' in a disastrous manner, losing

3-1 to Peru in front of 47,000 spectators in Cordoba.

Joe Jordan, once again, netted for the Scots inside the first 15 minutes after Peru's eccentric goalkeeper Quirogo, dubbed 'El Loco' parried skipper Bruce Rioch's shot into his path.

Cueto Cesar levelled things up just before the interval but then the usually reliable Don Masson missed a 62nd minute penalty and after that Scotland caved in. Cubillas netted two stunning goals late on as MacLeod's men ran round in circles.

There was a severe set back to MacLeod's plans after this game when the World Cup committee carried out a routine drugs test on two of the Scotland players. One of them, the West Bromwich Albion winger Willie Johnston, formerly of Rangers, was found to have taken some inexpensive yellow sugar-coated tablets, usually prescribed for 'mental and physical fatigue'. He was sent home immediately, his international career in tatters.

Johnston, in fact, was completely out of touch against Peru and Colin Malam, in his book World Cup Argentina stated that "Johnston's performance against Peru had been enough to give stimulants a bad name."

The incident threw the Scottish party into a state of shock. The SFA issued warnings to all the players not to take any sort of tablets or pills without telling the party's doctor.

It was no real surprise – after all that trauma - when a demoralised Scotland produced lack-lustre performance against a moderate Iran side in their next game.

Playing again in Cordoba, in front of 10,000 sun-drenched spectators, they drew 1-1, having expected to win hands down.

An own goal by centre-back Eskandarian two minutes before the break gave Scotland the lead, but after Manchester United defender Martin Buchan had gone off with a head injury early in the second half, the team lost its way. Danalfar equalised and although Scotland were still in with a good chance of moving through to the next stage of the competition, it was going to be much harder after this disappointing draw.

At this juncture, morale within the Scottish camp had reached an all-time low…and to make things worse, Chrysler withdrew the squad from its advertising campaign.

But the players buckled down to business. They wanted to show their supporters that they weren't as bad as everyone thought and they went into their game with Holland, the 1974 runners-up, with nothing to lose and everything to gain. Indeed, they had to go and out win, and win well, by at least three goals.

MacLeod's men went out, heads on high, and produced one of the best displays by a Scotland team for year's. They played superbly well and beat the Dutch 3-2.

With some 50,000 fans inside the Mendoza Stadium, Holland went ahead when Rensenbrink slammed home a penalty after Neeskens had been floored and carried off. This rocked the Scots back on their heels, but they responded and shortly before half-time drew level when Graeme Souness headed down for Kenny Dalglish to drive the ball past Jongbloed in the Dutch goal.

After the interval, Scotland pushed forward and were awarded a spot-kick themselves by fussy Austrian referee Linemayr. This time Gemmill stepped up to fire home, thus erasing the memories of Masson's miss in the previous game.

Scotland, playing with confidence, surged forward and on 68 minutes Gemmill produced a piece of magic. Cutting in from the right-wing, he wriggled past three defenders, switching the ball from his right foot to his left, to score a stunning, individual goal – one of the finest ever seen in World Cup football finals – and remember the competition had been going since 1930.

But three minutes later, Scotland's jubilant and chanting supporters were choked as Johnny Rep thumped in a shot from 25 yards to reduce the deficit. Scotland were down but not yet out. They fought to the end, Dalglish and Jordan both headed inches wide, but it was all over. A 3-2 defeat meant that brave Scotland had failed to make it through to the second stage yet again, eliminated at the first hurdle due to a lack of goals.

There's no doubt, they played as well as they could – better than ever against Holland - but one feels that their below-par performance against Peru ruined their chances of making progress.

How group 4 finished in the 1978 World Cup finals

Team	P	W	D	L	F	A	Pts
Peru	3	2	1	0	7	2	5
Netherlands	3	1	1	1	5	3	3
Scotland	3	1	1	1	5	6	3
Iran	3	0	1	2	2	8	1

Scotland headed off to sunny Spain for the 1982 World Cup finals with the former Celtic defender Jock Stein at the helm.

Could this be Scotland's year? The optimism was high and with a few more extra faces in the party, these 22 players set off in search of glory in the summer sun:

SQUAD LIST
WORLD CUP 1982 - SPAIN

1. Alan Rough   GK
2. Danny McGrain
3. Frank Gray
4. Graeme Souness
5. Alan Hansen
6. Willie Miller
7. Gordon Strachan
8. Kenny Dalglish
9. Alan Brazil
10. John Wark
11. John Robertson
12. George Wood   GK
13. Alex McLeish
14. David Narey
15. Joe Jordan
16. Asa Hartford
17. Alan Evans
18. Steve Archibald
19. Paul Sturrock
20. Davie Provan
21. George Burley
22. Jim Leighton   GK

Scotland team line-up against Belarus

Our first match on Group 'A' happened to be the opening fixture of the tournament against the reigning world champions, Brazil.

The scenery and the noise – there were 80,000 fans present inside the Saint-Denis Stadium - made me realise how big this competition is.

We went a goal down early on, Cesar Sampaio scoring after just four minutes, but we struck back on 38 minutes with a penalty from John Collins after I had been fouled inside the box.

Going in all-square at half-time, we thought we could win – given the breaks – and came mighty close to doing that, but an unfortunate own-goal, conceded by Tom Boyd with just over a quarter-of-an-hour remaining gave the Brazilians an undeserved 2-1 victory.

A 1-1 draw with Norway in front of more than 30,000 fans in Bordeaux where Craig Burley's 66th minute equaliser cancelled out Havaard Flo's opener just after half-time, opened up the group for us, and depending on how results went elsewhere, we could still qualify for the second stage if we could overcome Morocco in St Etienne.

Well, we put on an absolutely awful display in front of a full-house of 35,500. The team never got going, we were slap-happy with our passing, our shooting was completely off target and in the end were battered 3-0, Bassir (in the 22nd and 85th minutes) and Hadda (early in the second

half) scoring the decisive goals.

We got what our performance deserved – nothing – and it meant yet again, we were going home early.

The final Group 'A' table at the 1998 World Cup

Team	P	W	D	L	F	A	Pts
Brazil	3	2	0	1	6	3	6
Norway	3	1	2	0	5	4	5
Morocco	3	1	1	1	5	5	4
Scotland	3	0	1	2	2	6	1

Since their exploits in 1998, Scotland have failed to qualify for the last four major international competitions (two World Cups, two European Championships), two under Craig Brown and two under Berti Vogts.

Brown was replaced by Vogts who, in turn, lost out to Walter Smith.

Smith, to his credit, has started to develop a team that he believes will be capable of putting some much-needed pride back into Scottish football, something that has been missing for far too long.

Lorenzo Amoruso agrees,

"I think there has been quite good improvement already for the Scotland team under Walter Smith.

And I believe by leaving out some of the older players and introducing some of the youngsters, he will eventually find the right solution and get a decent squad together.

Obviously the best solution to change things on the pitch is for a fresh wind of young players to come good, all at the same time.

Football is so strange. A manager comes in with a great personality, a big smile, chirpy voice and nice attitude – but he simply can't blend with the players.

Walter can, and I believe he will, succeed in turning things round on the pitch for Scotland.

_Walter was the man who introduced to me

Tartan Turmoil
the fall and rise of Scottish Football

to Scottish football, signing me from Fiorentina in 1997, and as soon as I spoke to him, and the chairman, my mind was virtually made up.

And then, after having a chat with Walter on his own, I knew I was going to like Scotland and Glasgow. He was an absolute gentleman, the sort of man who really wanted to do well and that is the way I feel about him today. Scottish football is in safe hands, because Walter Smith is the right man for the job."

Although some of the senior professionals will be too old for the next championship campaign (Euro 2008), we now have a nice blend of youth and experience, players being guided along by Rangers' star Barry Ferguson, helped at the back by Craig Gordon and Andy Webster, a mature Darren Fletcher of Manchester United in midfield and with a very useful array of forwards who, it is hoped, will help out Kenny Miller.

It is a good reason to be optimistic about the future of Scottish football on the international circuit…because the next generation of players will have the responsibility of putting our country firmly back on the world football map.

Craig Gordon in action for Scotland

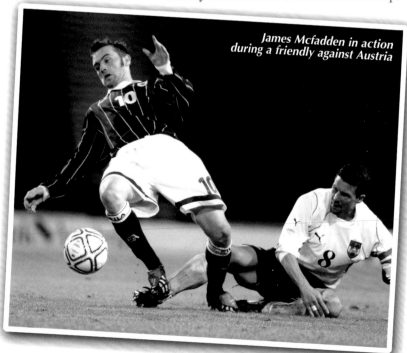

James Mcfadden in action during a friendly against Austria

These are the players – already used by manager Walter Smith - who, I feel, will form the basis of the Scotland senior squad over the next few years, injuries permitting of course:

1.	Rab Douglas	age 36
2.	Craig Gordon	age 23
3.	Andy Webster	age 23
4.	Christian Dailly	age 32
5.	David Weir	age 35
6.	Barry Ferguson	age 27
7.	Darren Fletcher	age 21
8.	Graeme Alexander	age 34
9.	Kenny Miller	age 26
10.	Paul Hartley	age 29
11.	Nigel Quashie	age 27

Tartan Turmoil
the fall and rise of Scottish Football

Of these 26 players, perhaps seven or eight will not take part in the next qualifications for the 2010 World Cup finals.

That leaves the basis of perhaps 18. So, looking towards the future, hopefully Smith can formulate a team good and strong enough to win a sufficient number of games that will get Scotland back on track and for starters into Euro 2008 (at least). After, it will be a case of introducing a few new faces, formulating a new system and hoping that the squad can gel together and produce the form that will enable the Tartan Army to march proudly and confidently all the way to the World Cup finals in 2010. Yes – the lads can do it….I'm confident of that.

Darren Fletcher and David Weir

12. Craig Beattie   age 21

13. Neil McCann   age 31

14. James McFadden   age 22

15. Steven Pressley   age 32

16. Gary Naysmith   age 27

17. Gary Caldwell   age 23

18. Steven Caldwell   age 25

19. Lee McCulloch   age 27

20. Gary O'Connor   age 21

21. Calum Davidson   age 29

22. Ian Murray   age 22

23. Shaun Maloney   age 22

24. Ryan Esson   age 25

25. Jackie McNamara   age 32

26. David Marshall   age 20

* Ages at 2006

SCOTLAND'S RI
THE WORLD SC

WORLD CUP

Scotland has participated in the final stages of eight World Cup tournaments, the details of which are as follows:

1954 – Switzerland

16 June	v. Austria (Zurich)	lost 1-0
19 June	v. Uruguay (Basle)	lost 7-0

1958 – Sweden

8 June	v. Yugoslavia (Vasteras)	drew 1-1
11 June	v. Paraguay (Norrkoping)	lost 3-2
15 June	v. France (Orebro)	lost 2-1

1974 – Germany

14 June	v. Zaire (Dortmund)	won 2-0
18 June	v. Brazil (Frankfurt)	drew 0-0
22 June	v. Yugoslavia (Frankfurt)	drew 1-1

1978 – Argentina

3 June	v. Peru (Cordoba)	lost 3-1
7 June	v. Iran (Cordoba)	drew 1-1
11 June	v. Netherlands (Mendoza)	won 3-2

1982 – Spain

15 June	v New Zealand (Malaga)	won 5-2
18 June	v. Brazil (Seville)	lost 4-1
22 June	v. USSR (Malaga)	drew 2-2

1986 – Mexico

4 June	v. Denmark (Neza)	lost 1-0
8 June	v. West Germany (Quertera)	lost 2-1
13 June	v. Uruguay (Neza)	drew 0-0

1990- Italy

11 June	v. Costa Rica (Genoa)	lost 1-0
16 June	v. Sweden (Genoa)	won 2-1
20 June	v. Brazil (Turin)	lost 1-0

1998 – France

10 June	v. Brazil (Paris)	lost 2-1
16 June	v. Norway (Bordeaux)	drew 1-1
23 June	v. Morocco (St Etienne)	lost 3-0

EUROPEAN CHAMPIONSHIPS

Scotland has competed in the final stages of the European Championship twice, the details of which are as follows:

1992 – Sweden

12 June	v. Netherlands (Gothenburg)	lost 1-0
15 June	v. Germany (Norrkoping)	lost 2-0
18 June	v. C.I.S. (Norrkoping)	won 3-0

1996 – England

10 June	v. Netherlands (Birmingham)	drew 0-0
15 June	v. England (London)	lost 2-0
18 June	v. Switzerland (Birmingham)	won 1-0

CORD ON
ENE

• *For the 2008 European Championships, Scotland have been drawn in group 'B' qualifiers along with Faroe Islands, France, Georgia, Italy, Lithuania and Ukraine.*

ROUS CUP
Scotland has played in the Rous Cup competition five times, details as follows:

25 May 1985	v. England	(Glasgow)	won 1-0
23 April 1986	v. England	(Wembley)	lost 2-1
23 May 1987	v. England	(Glasgow)	drew 0-0
26 May 1987	v. Brazil	(Glasgow)	lost 2-0
17 May 1988	v. Colombia	(Glasgow)	drew 0-0
21 May 1988	v. England	(Wembley)	lost 1-0
27 May 1989	v. England	(Glasgow)	lost 2-0
30 May 1989	v. Chile	(Glasgow)	won 2-0

BRITISH HOME INTERNATIONAL CHAMPIONSHIP
Scotland played in the last home international championship in 1982, the details being:

28 April	v. N Ireland	(Belfast)	drew 1-1
24 May	v. Wales	(Glasgow)	won 1-0
29 May	v. England	(Glasgow)	lost 1-0

KIRKIN CUP
Scotland won the Kirin Cup the first trophy for the national team in twenty years:

2006 - Japan

11 May	v. Bulgaria	(Kobe)	won 5-1
13 May	v. Japan	(Saitama)	drew 0-0

James McFadden in action for Scotland

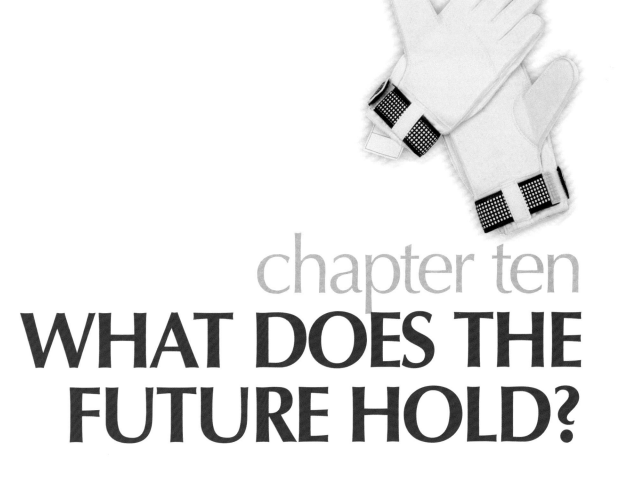

chapter ten

WHAT DOES THE FUTURE HOLD?

Walter Smith has a nation back on the edge of their seats; he has started to get the best results out of young players who only two years ago looked like frightened cats. If these young players can keep up their performance level on a match-to-match basis, the interest in Scottish football will be on the rise again. The kids have more interest in the game when the national team are playing well and individuals are catching the eyes of the nation.

They will be talking about these players and who they want to idolise at their school for the rest of their childhood. Not only, do we want kids to idolise our players, we want them to aspire to become one of them in the future. If we want to get them to play the game, we have to start producing and advancing facilities for them.

To make progress on the World Scene we will have to start back at the grass roots level because that's where there needs to be a lot of changes.

If we are to get an influx of new talent, there has to be changes. At schoolboy, amateur and recreational level. Good coaching and training should start early.

Is anybody doing anything about it? That's the big question for Scottish football.

Well, the answer is yes, the SFA and other bodies are working hard at trying to get the sport back on track, but they need help from the financial bodies. Having lost out on the chance to play in the World Cup in Germany, not only have the players lost out on bonuses and the experience of a lifetime, but the Scottish Football Association has lost out on a cash windfall. The monies they received after the 1998 World cup in France was recorded in their accounts as over £1m after player fees, travel, accommodation, security and promotional activities.

This was not distributed in isolation as a windfall, but went into the general revenue of the SFA for that year. This allowed the SFA to make a bigger than usual contribution to the football trust (£1m rather than the usual £0.5M) which was the most efficient way of investing in facilities and distributing money to clubs for their youth schemes.

Missing out on all the big competitions does make it harder to put monies into grass roots, so the better the National team does in World Cups and European Championships the more money the SFA can contribute to the lower end of the football ladder. In March 2004 a Youth Action Plan, for Scottish Football was unveiled at Hampden Park by SFA Chief Executive David Taylor and the then Minister for Tourism, Culture and Sport, Frank McAveety.

The Scottish Football Association (SFA), together with the Scottish Executive and **sportscotland**, launched a £31m Action Plan to increase the number of players in

David Taylor
Chief Executive, The Scottish F.A.

Scotland and raise standards at all levels of the game.

The Action Plan makes wide-ranging changes to the way the youth game in Scotland will be organised and financed over the next 10 years. It is a far-reaching bid to raise participation in the game and improve the competitive standards across all age groups, from the game's grass roots to the national team. It is the outcome of the most comprehensive and independent review of youth football ever undertaken in the UK. More than 200 individuals and organisations contributed to the review over an 18-month period and its findings now form the basis for the Action Plan that is now being implemented.

Significantly, the plan now has a long-term funding strategy in place. The SFA will contribute £10m towards its running over 10 years, supported by Government funding of £12m managed by **sportscotland**. A further £9m is currently being invested in community programmes by the SFA and local authorities will be used to support the Action Plan. For years we have been held back in Scotland by lack of investment.

With a great deal of hard work we are now beginning to see young players with the potential to come through the ranks and become the basis of our International squad in the future. Now is the time to recognise that these players are our future, and devote sufficient resources to youth development to enable our International team to qualify for World Cup Finals and European Championships, as we have done in the past.

The SFA's Chief Executive, David Taylor, welcomed the launch of the Plan in 2004 saying, *"The Action Plan presents us with a clear and cohesive way forward, backed by a viable and robust funding strategy. It has evolved through independent consultation, engaging everyone who cares about the future of the Scottish game - from the parents and coaches on the touchline to the national coach and the top clubs.*

"We are now in a position to make real progress, providing more opportunities for young people to play the game in Scotland. This will lay the foundation for clubs and national teams at the performance end of the game, so Scotland can get back to qualifying for major tournaments."

Changes at grass roots levels will see support and investment provided to schools to increase participation, and to youth football clubs to strengthen club and community development.

sportscotland's involvement in football will assist with the changes that are needed by:

- Achieving excellence in sport in order to be able to compete at the highest international level.

- Promoting sport as part of an active lifestyle and encouraging individuals to develop and achieve their potential in the game.

- Developing facilities in Scotland to play and practice the game.

- Proactively increasing press coverage by helping the media to understand the needs of Scottish football.

- Widening opportunities to increase participation in the game, particularly by those currently excluded.

As former Chief Executive of **sportscotland**, Ian Robson said at the launch of the plan:

"Scottish players are currently standing at 3.6% of the population, which is less than half that of similar countries like Holland and Norway."

We also have one of the lowest ratio of players per club at 23 on average.

This shows that we have a high number of one-team clubs - unlike our continental rivals whose 'community club' structures boast player averages in excess of 300. At the heart of the Action Plan is the desire to increase player participation in Scotland by at least 20%.

A new Quality Mark scheme will see the

We want to see more kids involved in the sport with clear means of progressing through the ranks. This country has a significant number of organisations involved in youth football and while they are all doing great work we need to see some joined-up thinking

David Taylor Chief Executive, The Scottish F.A.

SFA work with clubs and schools at grass roots to encourage best practice in volunteer, coach and player development. The new strategy will also attract volunteers to support and to get more young people to play the game. The new and simplified National Registration System for players over 12 years of age will do away with excessive paperwork, making it easier for more young footballers to get involved.

Football is our main sport but we have to learn from the comparative success of other European nations, especially countries of a similar size to Scotland. Scotland has one of the lowest numbers of players as a percentage of population in Europe.

These are fundamental issues that we need to overcome if our national teams are to perform consistently and successfully on World and European stages.

healthier.

SFA Project Implementation Manager Alan MacNab, who brings many years experience in project management from the business world, continues to put together a team that will implement the plan. Alan who played junior football for more than 10 years, representing Linlithglow Rose and Cumbernauld United said in April 2006 that the past months and years had been about "building relationships, identifying budgets and establishing committees, (to deliver the Action Plan)"

Six regional managers, spread geographically across Scotland, are responsible for supervising the running of the scheme.

Former Aberdeen, Hibernian and Airdrieonians player Tommy McIntyre assists Alan as Head of Youth Development.

Tommy is responsible for developing grass roots football and the technical development of the Youth Initiative Programme. Tommy acts as an adviser in youth football programmes to the new regional network.

Jim Fleeting, who has been the architect of the SFA Community Coaches Scheme, takes over as Head of Regional Programmes and Tommy Wilson has been promoted to Head of Coaching and will also look after the U19 International team.

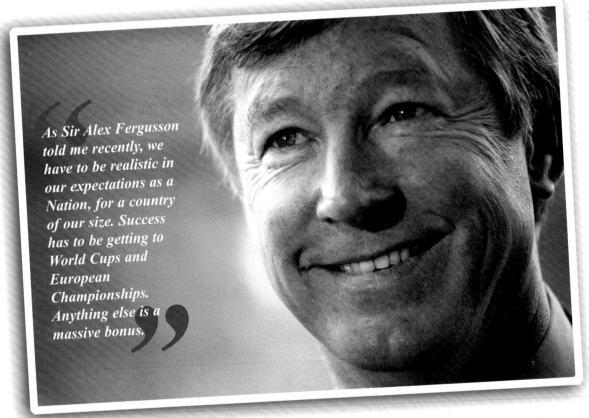

> *As Sir Alex Fergusson told me recently, we have to be realistic in our expectations as a Nation, for a country of our size. Success has to be getting to World Cups and European Championships. Anything else is a massive bonus.*

The new structure that is being put in place, on a local and national level, will encourage more young people to take part in regular physical activity and make them

Sheila Begbie has taken up a position as Head of the Women's Business Unit, to reflect the continued emphasis on the development of womens' and girls' football. Most members of staff will now have wider responsibilities, but the delivery of the Action Plan is of vital importance to get the game moving forward again. The SFA has now taken over responsibility for the Under 16 national squad from the Scottish Schools' Football Association.

Scotlands' U17 squad lines up vs Faroe Islands

One of the major features of this programme is international competition in the Under 16 Victory Shield tournament, which sees Scotland play against England, Wales and Northern Ireland.

The programme's long-term aim is the development of players to prepare them for club competitions and future national teams. This system is already reaping the benefits as our Under 17 and Under 19 international teams had both qualified for the Elite Final Qualification Round for the 2005, UEFA U17 and U19 Championships. The Action Plan will create a structure allowing a clear route of progression for all young footballers in Scotland.

To succeed, the Action Plan needs additional external funding and relies on sponsorship income. The Bank of Scotland recently promised £1.5m over the next three years.

The proof of the pudding, will be when we see a steady flow of talented young footballers progress to our National side.

We still have to re-create an environment where anyone has the opportunity to be able to play football at anytime. This was always part and parcel of our working class life and something we took for granted. That's what football was about,

whether there were just two of you and you just shot at the goal or whether there were twelve of you.

That was just what we did.

Building housing estates with no outside facilities for the kids has destroyed the game. We need to act quickly to reverse these trends, to provide a safe area that players of the future can develop their basic skills in, so they can become successful at a higher level of the game.

We need to recreate the atmosphere, which you could almost 'touch' on the streets, on the playing fields and in schools. The kids today have too many distractions, computer games, play-stations, etc., some of them are passionate about football but do not have the incentive to go out and play the game.

If we think back to how much time we spent playing football when we were kids it probably amounted to six days a week. We played football morning, noon and night and during all the holidays. To recreate that in this day an age might not prove viable. We could offer structured coaching sessions for children for six days a week. Each session might only cost a few pounds, but over the course of the week this might prove too expensive for most families. Therefore, we find ourselves back to the scenario, where kids still do not have the opportunity to play football often enough.

Unfortunately, this highlights how football is now catching up with other sports where funding from parents often dictates how far our children can develop in their selected sport. This is the main problem with developing gifted sports people in this country. Children nowadays play maybe a

In short, we have to try and recreate park and street football facilities, whether being indoor or outdoor, or we will remain in decline as a footballing nation. We must be patient and start to develop the game with children from the age of 6 or 7. It will take ten years before we see the results at the professional level of the game.

With the new initiatives being introduced, football clubs at all levels should benefit and hopefully with new facilities kids can

Ian Wilson tangles with Chris Waddle back in 1987 at Hampden Park

tenth of what we did and therefore progress is slower. The rot has set in and we need to design safe areas for children to go and play football. Indoor areas can be used all year round but must be made available at a subsidised cost that all families can afford.

once again develop their talent for the game and maybe one of these clubs will find the "new Kenny Dalglish".

So what does the future hold?

With the structured approach of the Action Plan and adequate funding in Scotland it will provide clubs, at all levels, with the

Kevin Gallacher in action during a game with Belarus

This is what they tried with some success and goes all the way back in time.

We talk about the great players like Baxter, Law and Dalglish, players with great individual talent, but through the years football has developed more into a team game. Players have lost that little bit of individualism.

My own personal hope for the future is that when I travel home to visit my family in Scotland I will see kids enjoying playing football once again in the newly purpose built facilities.

opportunity to discover, nurture and develop football talent. People must also start to pay more attention to the recreational side of the game again, so that we are able to produce not just a higher level of player, but more players available to the professional game.

This will provide the manager of our National side with the quality needed to compete on the international scene.

Moving on from this period of turmoil, things seem to be settling down, and with renewed ambition from within the Scottish game we can only hope that this drives better competition in the Scottish Leagues. At international level, we must hope that firstly we can enjoy some initial successes, and I don't just look at that from a materialistic point of view. I think that as long as Scotland are challenging for European Championships and the World Cup on a regular basis then the game as whole will benefit.

I first got my international call up way back in 1987 and the squads that both Andy Roxburgh and Craig Brown selected were based on a mixture of star names with the professional hard working footballer. Their theory seemed to be, if they could take team spirit that they had in club football and bring it into the international set up, results would come.

chapter eleven

EUROPEAN CHAMPIONSHIPS 2008

The fact that we did not qualify for the 2006 World Cup in Germany is in the past. The Tartan Army, like all the guys in Walter Smith's squad, were rivoted to their TV screens for the draw for the 2008 European Championship Qualifiers. This took place on 27th January, 2006, in Montreux, Switzerland.

There were 7 pots with different countries named on each ball, Scotland were put in pot 4 with Bosnia-Herzegovina, Republic of Ireland, Belgium, Latvia, Israel and Slovenia.

Being put in pot 4 meant we would have a harder task as we would have three of the better nations in the same group.

The hardest part about these draws is the waiting.

Northern Ireland were the first British team to be selected and put into group F, Wales were next followed by Scotland who joined Lithuania, Georgia and Faroe Islands in group B.

Not a bad start I first thought but with three of the better countries still to be drawn out and added to our group, I just had to sit and keep my fingers crossed for a bit of luck.

Unfortunately as Ukraine, Italy and France were drawn in our group our luck ran out.

We have drawn the Faroe Islands and Lithuania in our last two European qualifying groups. As for the Faroe Islands, what can I say? On paper they shouldn't cause any problems, but in the last two European qualifiers they gave us a scare, especially away from home where we have only managed to draw with them.

Although the Faroe Islands have a new stadium, we do not know yet whether we will play in the old one which has some bad memories for us. We now have the opportunity to 'bury the ghosts of the past'.

We start the campaign at Hampden Park against the Faroe Islanders and should end up with maximum points.

Georgia are a team we have never met at international level before. They also failed to qualify for the World Cup in Germany. The game in Georgia may prove to be tough, but we should collect the points at Hampden in March 2007.

Lithuania are very similar to the Georgians and they will make it difficult on their own pitch, but they don't travel too well. They did managed to take three points off us in our last European championship meeting away in Lithuania and made us fight for our return 1-0 win. We should take maximum points out of both games against Lithuania.

We could be top of the group by the end of September 2006 with a home game against the Faroe Islands and an away game against Lithuania.

We have never met the Ukraine in any competition before and they will be no easy turn over. Ukraine qualified for the World Cup in Germany by topping their group which contained European champions Greece!!!

Like all eastern European countries they may struggle away from home. We meet them in October 2006 followed by a double-header firstly with France at home and then the Ukrainians, these games could decide our fate.

When Italy came out of the hat I knew it was going to be difficult. We recently played against them in the World Cup qualifiers, where we gave a good account of ourselves in both matches. But can we raise the bar again and beat them now? They have a team full of superstars. It will be a tough call and I will watch with anticipation.

Playing them last in the group could be a good omen. If it goes down to the wire, the Italians might have qualified by the last game and rest some of the superstars.

To finally pull former World Champions, France out of the hat, was the straw that broke the camels back!!!

They have struggled of late, but getting the old stars like Zidane back from

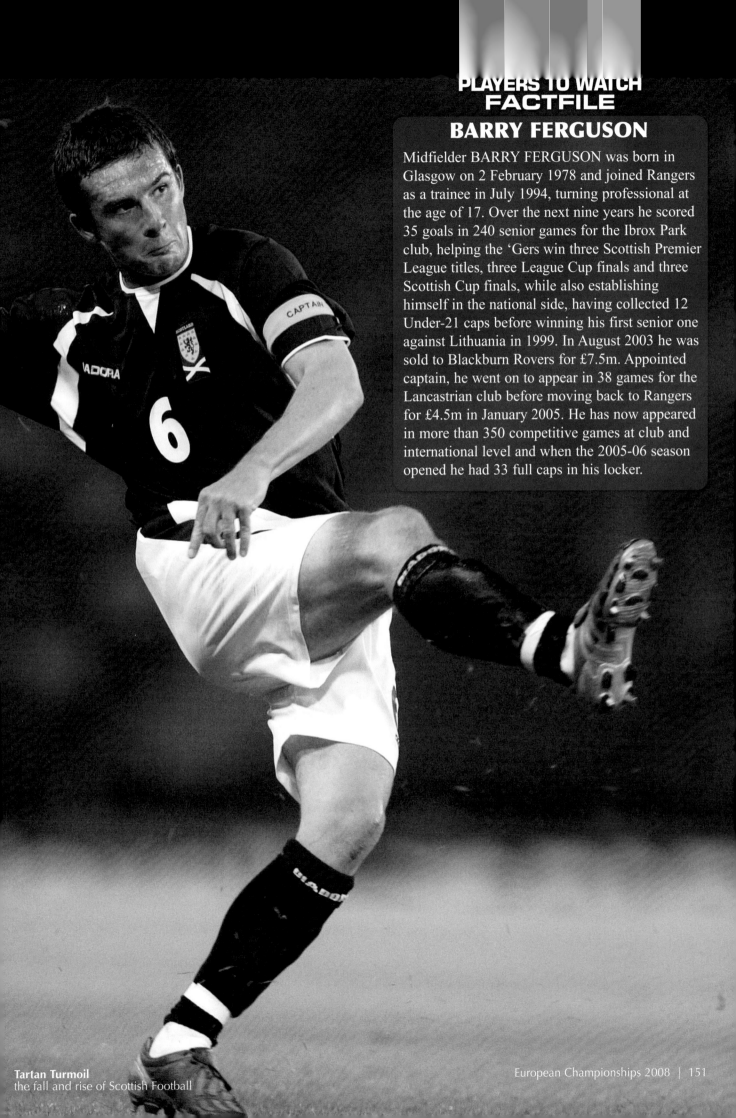

BARRY FERGUSON

Midfielder BARRY FERGUSON was born in Glasgow on 2 February 1978 and joined Rangers as a trainee in July 1994, turning professional at the age of 17. Over the next nine years he scored 35 goals in 240 senior games for the Ibrox Park club, helping the 'Gers win three Scottish Premier League titles, three League Cup finals and three Scottish Cup finals, while also establishing himself in the national side, having collected 12 Under-21 caps before winning his first senior one against Lithuania in 1999. In August 2003 he was sold to Blackburn Rovers for £7.5m. Appointed captain, he went on to appear in 38 games for the Lancastrian club before moving back to Rangers for £4.5m in January 2005. He has now appeared in more than 350 competitive games at club and international level and when the 2005-06 season opened he had 33 full caps in his locker.

Tartan Turmoil
the fall and rise of Scottish Football

PLAYERS TO WATCH
FACTFILE
DARREN FLETCHER

Midfielder DARREN FLETCHER, six feet tall, was born in Edinburgh on 1 February 1984 and graduated through the ranks at Old Trafford before signing as a full-time professional in February 2001. He has so far represented Scotland at three different levels, gaining one 'B', two Under-21 and 19 full caps; he was an FA Cup winner with the Reds in 2004 and has now played in well over 100 senior games for Manchester United.

Tartan Turmoil
the fall and rise of Scottish Football

retirement helped them qualify for the World Cup. Like us, they are going through a re-building period. The new players are still trying to adjust to the standard the French have set. Hopefully when we meet them at Hampden in October 2006 they will be struggling to find form!!!!

We live in anticipation, as a proud nation, that on our day we are capable of beating the BEST. Our history has been written by our heroes, Law, Dalglish, Souness and many others.

SCOTLAND'S OPPONENTS IN THE 2008 EUROPEAN CHAMPIONSHIP QUALIFIERS:

- **Faroe Islands**
- **France**
- **Georgia**
- **Italy**
- **Lithuania**
- **Ukraine**

Members of FIFA since 1988, the FAROE ISLANDS have featured in the FIFA World Cup qualifiers since 1994, as yet with no serious prospect of qualifying. In the preliminary tournament for the 2002 FIFA World Cup their only wins came against Luxembourg as opponents like Russia, Slovenia and Switzerland proved too strong.

Classier opposition also proved their downfall in previous qualifying competitions. But the Faroe Islands take the credit for one major upset in a 1990 European Championships qualifier, when they beat a strong Austrian side 1-0 on neutral ground in Sweden.

In the qualifiers for Euro 2004, Scotland and Germany encountered surprisingly tough opposition from the Faroe Islands. The Scots were lucky to scramble a 2-2 away draw in September 2002 while in their away leg, the dignity of Germany was only saved by two late goals as they squeezed out a 2-1 victory. Even at home,

the Germans struggled to impose themselves on the minnows.

Experienced striker John Peterson scored both goals against Scotland in the 2004 qualifying stages and is likely to be lining up for the Faroe Islands again.

A forceful player, good in the air, he has been on the international scene for six years and in that time has given several quality defenders plenty to think about.

Another player Scotland will have to be aware of is Peterson's co-striker Hjalgrim Elltor who hit the post in the dying minutes. He was placed in a one-on-one situation with the German goalkeeper Oliver Kahn in the above mentioned qualifying game. If Elltor had found the mark he would have punished a profligate German team who should have been comfortably ahead by that stage. And at the same time may well have been given the freedom of the Faroe Islands (even a knighthood).

Between them Messrs Elltor and Peterson could cause a few problems – beware.

FRANCE has twice won the European Championship, beating Spain 2-0 in 1984 and Italy 2-1 in sudden death in 2000. They have also won the World Cup, beating Brazil 3-0 in 1998.

Members of FIFA since 1904, the country hosted the first European Cup final in 1956. Legendary striker Juste Fontaine holds the record for scoring most goals in the finals of a World Cup tournament (13 in 1958) and Frenchman Jules Rimet, who served as FIFA president for over 20 years, was instrumental in creating the World Cup.

Of the current playing squad, Thierry Henry will, for sure, be the star performer in the French attack. Arsenal's all-time

The French team line up

record marksman, he moved to Highbury for £8m in 1999 from Juventus having started his career with AS Monaco. He has netted well over 300 goals in a wonderful career, helping the Gunners win two Premiership titles and two FA Cup finals. He has so far gained 75 caps for France.

Hoping to create the openings for Henry will be midfielder Zinedine Zindane, European 'Player of the Year' in 1998 and World 'Player of the Year' in 1998, 2000 and 2003. He joined his present club, Real Madrid, for a record fee of £45.6m in 2001, having previously starred for Cannes, Bordeaux and Juventus. He won League and Cup medals in Italy and Spain, has 90 caps to his credit and helped France win the European Championship and World Cup.

GEORGIA, members of FIFA since 1992, will be tough opponents. They have several quality players, many of whom are plying their trade in other countries. Among those who will be hoping to make an impact in the European qualifiers are 26 year-old striker Levn Melkadze (now with Valerenga) and 18 year-old midfielder Levan Tskitischvili (currently with the German side Wolfsburg).

Both players helped Tbilisi win the Georgian League title in 2005 while Melkadze finished up as the leading marksman with 27 goals.

ITALY, European Champion winners in 1968 v. Yugoslavia and beaten finalists v. France in 2000, has also won the World Cup three times, in 1934 1938 and 1982.

Members of FIFA since 1905, they are one of the favourites to do well in Euro' 2008 but at the moment they are not producing the results expected of them at international level.

Two players who the Italians hope will prosper are forwards Alessandro Del Piero and Francesco Totti.

Del Piero, born in Conegliano, Treviso in November 1974, played for Padova before joining Juventus for whom he made his debut in Serie 'A' in 1993. The recipient of six Italian League winner's medals, one Cup winner's medal and a Champions League winner's prize (all with Juventus), he has now scored over 25 goals in more than 60 internationals for Italy. A brilliant ball player, sharp and incisive, he can turn a game on its' head with one piece of magic.

Totti was born in the Chinese Year of the Dragon, September 1976 in Rome. A creator as well as a scorer of goals - not least from free kicks – he can operate from a variety of attacking positions but it is in the free role behind the strikers that his skill and technique are best showcased. He is widely regarded as one of the finest players in the modern game.

PLAYERS TO WATCH FACTFILE
CRAIG GORDON

Goalkeeper CRAIG GORDON, 6ft 4ins tall and over 13st in weight, was born in Edinburgh on 31 December 1982. He signed initially for Hearts as a schoolboy at the age of 12, progressing through the various channels before signing professional forms in 1999. He was loaned out to Cowdenbeath before making his senior debut for Hearts v. Livingston in October 2002, having earlier helped the Tynecastle club win both the Scottish Youth Cup and Youth League. Voted Scotland's 'Young Player of the Year' he had an outstanding 2003-04 season, gaining his first full cap v. Trinidad & Tobago at the end of that campaign. He's now played in ten full, two 'B' and five Under-21 internationals and has 150 club appearances safely under his belt.

PLAYERS TO WATCH
FACTFILE
JAMES McFADDEN

JAMES McFADDEN is an out-and-out winger who can also play through the middle if required. Born in Glasgow on 14 April 1983, he joined Motherwell straight from school, turned professional at the first opportunity and proceeded to score 32 goals in only 70 games for the Fir Park club before joining Everton for £1.25m in September 2003. Capped 25 times by Scotland at senior level, on seven occasions by the Under-21s and once for the 'B' team, he has now netted half-a-dozen times in 90 games for the Merseysiders.

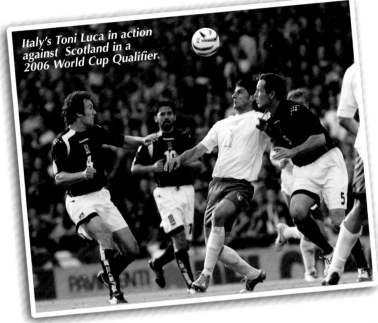

Italy's Toni Luca in action against Scotland in a 2006 World Cup Qualifier.

fine players and will be tough opponents this time round.

Striker Andriy Shevchenko, 29 from Kiev, is the one to watch out for. Voted European 'Footballer of the Year' in 2004 and the World's greatest player in 2005, he has scored 28 times in 63 internationals for Ukraine and currently lies second (to the legendary Gunnar Nordhal) in AC Milan's all-time scoring charts with 125 goals.

He joined AS Roma as a professional in 1993 and has now scored 110 goals in 310 games for the Italian club, gaining winner's medals for Serie 'A' and European Super Cup triumphs in 2001, while also gaining almost 50 caps at senior level. He is known in Italy as the 'Roman God of the Football Pitch.'

LITHUANIA initially joined FIFA in 1923, dropped out and reclaimed status in 1992. They have done nothing out of the ordinary, although they did reasonably well in the qualifying rounds of the 1994 World Cup.

Two of the country's star players are midfielder Igoris Morinas and defender Tomas Zvirgzdauskas.

Morinas is now registered with FSV Mainz (Germany), having previously played for Hannover 96 in the Bundesliga. He has scored five goals in 29 full internationals.

Zvirgzdauskas, currently with Halmstads (Sweden) is strong and solid and he too has 29 full caps under his belt.

UKRAINE a member of FIFA since 1992, they posed little threat in Euro' 96 (4th in group 4), finished second in the same group (to France) in 2000 and came next to bottom in group 5 in 2004, but nevertheless they have some exceptionally

He joined Milan for £26m in 1999 and has two Serie 'A', European Cup and Champions League winner's medals to his credit. He turned down a big-money move to Chelsea in 2005.

Dynamo Kiev's 27 year-old Vladyslav Vashcuk – the subject of a forgery scandal a few year ago – will compete hard and long in midfield. An experienced international, in the past he has matched up with many of the world's finest in his position.

Andriy Shevchenko

Working on this book has been a bit of a quest for me. And without the help of countless people, I could not have got this far. The over-riding feeling I have, is that, despite the problems and setbacks of the last five or six years, there is still a feeling of optimism.

Behind the scenes, the Scottish FA is finally putting into place a strategy that will benefit clubs from grass roots to the SPL. And if any team needed encouragement, they need look no further than little Gretna. Playing Unibond League football six year's ago, they have progressed beyond belief. They have won back to back promotions, have made the

Final of the Scottish Cup and this is based on a largely Scottish squad. Not bad for a town with just 3,000 folk!

As for the international side, Walter Smith is beginning to build his squad for Euro 2008 based on younger players. I have highlighted some of the stars of the future to illustrate how promising things look. The recent results out in Japan were encouraging, and Walter Smith and his fledgling squad are to be congratulated for winning the 'Kirin Cup'

Looking at the group for Euro 2008, I can honestly see us getting enough points to qualify, and to make every Scotsman proud of his team once more.

"Walter Smith's 'heroes' did us proud in Japan in May 2006. He has restored our belief, in the games that he has been in charge, that we CAN compete once again on the International scene. Winning The Kirin Cup re-inforces my belief that under his stewardship we are building a squad of guys that can make the Tartan Army proud.

KEVIN GALLACHER"

PLAYERS TO WATCH
FACTFILE
KENNY MILLER

Striker KENNY MILLER agreed to move to Parkhead for the 2006-07 season and thus becomes only the third player to represent both Celtic and Rangers since WW2 – the others being Mo Johnston and Alfie Conn. Born in Edinburgh on 23 December 1979, he played for Hutchison Vale Boys Club before joining Hibernian in May 1996. He scored 14 goals in 53 games for the Easter Road club and eight in 11 starts when on loan to Stenhousemuir in 1998. He was signed by Rangers for £2m in July 2000 and in his first season at Ibrox Park notched 11 goals in 39 appearances before joining Wolves, initially on loan, signing permanently for £3m in December 2001. He twice finished as top-scorer at Molineux, helping the Wanderers reach the Premiership in 2004. He has one 'B', 22 full and seven Under-21 caps to his name.

Acknowledgements

I would like to thank the following for their help in the research for this book:

The Scottish FA

Lorenzo Amoruso

Walter Smith

Craig Brown CBE

Jim McLean

Kenny Dalglish

Sir Alex Ferguson

David Moyes

Graeme Souness

David Lee

Alan McNab

David Taylor, Chief Executive, The Scottish FA

Peter Rundo - *Photos, Fotopress, Dundee*

David Martin - *Photos*

Action Images - *Photos*

Tony Matthews - *Historian and Statistician*

John Booth

George Moss

Paul Jones - *Layout & Design*

Tartan Turmoil
the fall and rise of Scottish Football